Contents

Preface

One of the very first divisions to be formed by President Toda, was the Women's Division. It was created by him on 10 June, just a month after his inauguration as the second president of the Soka Gakkai.

On that occasion he said, "The ability of women is much greater than is usually thought. A western philosopher once said, 'Liquor is strong, the king stronger, women even more so, while the truth is the strongest of all.'" . . . "Since you are ready to pour your whole energy into kosen-rufu, I hope each of you will leave your name to posterity as one of the brilliant women in the history of the dissemination of Nichiren Daishonin's Buddhism. I hope you believe that this effort promises all good fortune and prosperity for your husbands and children. With such an important mission, you are completely different from and much nobler than those women whom people think to be rich and classy." (*The Human Revolution*, vol. 5, 210-11)

Women who have a sound philosophy in life possess the strength and optimism that ensures that they are undefeated by any adversity.

We are eternally grateful to Soka Gakkai International's current president, Daisaku Ikeda for filling us with courage by reminding us again and again that women possess an awe-inspiring power and a noble mission. He believes that "the victory of the Women's Division is the victory of Soka".

A very sincere effort has been made to compile President Ikeda's poems, essays, editorials and other guidances that would encourage members of the women's division. They provide a practical way forward on how to deal with a variety of issues and help us lead a fulfilled, meaningful and victorious life.

The publication of this book, aptly titled *Flowers of Hope* is a very precious gift to the women of Soka.

Cherishing this, let us cheerfully strive to create a new age with fresh spirits, fresh emotions and a powerful solidarity. United in the shared commitment of mentor and disciple, let us open a fresh page of dynamic development towards the new era of worldwide kosen-rufu.

Finally, let me express my deepest gratitude to Eternal Ganges and to all whose tireless efforts made this book possible.

Chabi Prasad
All India Women's Division Chief
Bharat Soka Gakkai
18 November 2013

Five Eternal Guidelines for the Women's Division

Everything begins with prayer

Advancing harmoniously with our families

Fostering young successors

Cherishing our communities and societies

Joyfully sharing our experiences in faith

Editorials

Soka Women Are the Sun of Time Without Beginning

All heavenly deities praise
and all Buddhas support
the activities
of our great women
Bodhisattvas of the Earth.

The Russian author Maxim Gorky (1868–1936), among whose famous works is the novel *Mother,* wrote: "Let us raise our voices in praise of woman, the Mother, inexhaustible fount of all-conquering life!"[1] As long as we, as human beings, have a profound appreciation and respect for the dedicated efforts of women—especially, the noble sincerity of mothers—we can advance vigorously on the correct path of life. Those who show themselves to be treacherous and disloyal are invariably individuals who also treat women with contempt, rudeness, and disrespect.

In the momentous undertaking of kosen-rufu, the earnest prayers and actions of our women's and young women's division members are an "inexhaustible fount" of victory. My wife and I would like to thank them for their admirable endeavours again this past year.

You are sure to
vibrantly adorn
the century of women,
wearing the jewelled crown
of truth and happiness.

The purpose of life is to become happy. To become happy, we must fight for truth and justice. And our Buddhist practice represents the most essential effort towards that end.

In a letter to one of his female disciples, Nichinyo, the Daishonin writes:

> Never seek this Gohonzon outside yourself. The Gohonzon exists only within the mortal flesh of us ordinary people who embrace the Lotus Sutra and chant Nam-myoho-renge-kyo. The body is the palace of the ninth consciousness [the pure, undefiled Buddha nature],[2] the unchanging reality that reigns over all of life's functions. ('The Real Aspect of the Gohonzon', WND-1, 832)

The sun of life of time without beginning shines in the hearts of Soka women. My mentor, second Soka Gakkai president Josei Toda, proclaimed a great turning point in the long history of women weeping at the hands of fate:

Women who embrace and uphold the Mystic Law are the most noble women of all. In what form will the proof of your practice of the Mystic Law flower in your lives in the future? Each of you in the end will experience without fail the blossoming of your own unique and ideal flower of happiness. That is the incredible power of faith in the Gohonzon.

Lightly embracing
even despairing circumstances—
how noble are mothers!

In a letter to the lay nun Myoichi, the Daishonin assures her:

Those who believe in the Lotus Sutra are as if in winter, but winter always turns to spring. Never, from ancient times on, has anyone heard or seen of winter turning back to autumn. Nor have we ever heard of a believer in the Lotus Sutra who turned into an ordinary [unenlightened] person. ('Winter Always Turns into Spring', WND-1, 536)

Myoichi's husband had preceded her in death, and she was left alone to care for their two children, one of whom was sickly. In the midst of this adversity, however, she remained true to the Daishonin's teachings.

Life is a never-ending struggle. The greater our mission, the more daunting the obstacles and difficulties that beset us. But where the encouragement of wise women resonates and the bright smiles of mothers shine, the darkness of sorrow and pessimism evaporates and gives way to a fragrant spring breeze of victory.

The Swiss philosopher Carl Hilty (1833–1909) observed: "Vanity is always noticed and pleases no one."[3] There is no need to put on airs or pretend to be better than you are. We are all human beings, and no one can be anything greater than a human being. The lives of those who take action for the sake of others and for the sake of the Law, just as they are and in the way most natural for them, are the most beautiful.

Our successors in the young women's division, with Buddhist study as their foundation, are reaching out to others in dialogue and thereby illuminating the darkness of these uncertain times with the bright light of hope. They are acting like "a lantern lighting up a place that has been dark for a hundred, a thousand, or ten thousand years" ('The One Essential Phrase', WND-1, 923), as described in the Gosho.

Madame Laureana San Pedro Rosales, the founder of Capitol University in the Philippines, declared that Soka women represent a vital presence in this troubled world and expressed her hopes for the continued global development of our network. She further voiced her wish that the ranks of Soka women dedicated to spreading the Buddhist message of peace would grow throughout the world and make the world a better place.

May the bright, sunny advance of our Soka women—watched by people round the globe—brim with boundless joy!

> The united efforts
> of the women's and young women's divisions
> have finally brought an age when
> kosen-rufu advances ever more dynamically,
> each person shining with happiness.

(*Value Creation*, December 2007, 7-31)

Notes:

1. M. Gorky, *Tales of Italy*, translated by Rose Prokofieva (Moscow: Foreign Languages Publishing House, n.d.), 75.

2. The ninth consciousness or the amala-consciousness, is the Buddha nature or the fundamental purifying force, that is free from all karmic impediments. Here, the Daishonin is associating it with Nam-myoho-renge-kyo.

3. Translated from German. Carl Hilty, *Für Schlaflose Nächte* (For Sleepless Nights), edited by Werner Braselmann (Freiburg: Herderbücherei, 1991), 92, May 24.

A Jewelled Crown of Happiness for the Women's Division[1]

Our admirable
women's division,
foremost in all the world,
possessing a wealth of good fortune
and a noble mission.

Untold numbers of women throughout the course of history have endured terrible suffering as a result of cruel wars, oppression, and the vagaries of destiny.

The aim of the Soka Century of Women, however, is to put an end to this cycle of sorrow and to give rise to an infinite blossoming of smiles across the globe, nurtured by peace, respect and happiness. A new age of hope that was once a distant dream has now begun.

Among Nichiren Daishonin's female followers was the lay nun Konichi, who had lost not only her husband but also the son she had greatly relied on. With the Daishonin's encouragement, however, she continued to dedicate herself steadfastly to her Buddhist practice. To this sincere follower whom he called the "Honorable Konichi," the Daishonin wrote: "In your present existence you have cast off the bonds of the three obediences;[2] already you have freed yourself from the hindrance of the five obstacles.[3] The moon of your mind [i.e., of your Buddha nature] is without shadow and all stain has vanished from your body. You are a Buddha in your present body—how wonderful, how wonderful!" ('Reply to the Lay Nun Kōnichi', WND-2, 1068).

The "three obediences" and the "five obstacles" refer to the restrictions and shackles that for centuries unfairly oppressed and caused suffering to women.

However, no matter what our circumstances, all of us, by chanting Nam-myoho-renge-kyo and courageously taking action for kosen-rufu, can definitely manifest the life-state of Buddhahood, resembling a beautiful full moon shining serenely in the skies of our heart. Filled with joy at knowing that we, just as we are, are supremely respect-worthy entities of the Mystic Law, we can confidently tap the wisdom and power of the Buddha to never be defeated by anything.

As the Daishonin teaches, we can transform karma into mission, and awaken from the state of ordinary people simply waiting to be saved to Bodhisattvas of the Earth dedicated to actively striving alongside our mentor to help others attain enlightenment, thereby realising happiness for ourselves and others.

None are demonstrating this more eloquently than our peerless women's division members.

At the Osaka Rally[4]of 1957, there was a women's division member who stood among the large crowd of members outside the packed Nakanoshima Civic Hall and listened to the speeches being broadcast over loudspeakers. Undaunted by the pouring rain and thunder, she engraved in her heart my declaration that the correct teaching of Nichiren Daishonin's Buddhism would definitely prevail.

This women's division member went on to overcome tragic loss and other harrowing trials—including the death of one of her young sons following an automobile accident, the family business falling into heavy debt and her personal battle with cancer. Today, her life is filled with fragrant flowers of victory.

Deeply trusted by the members of her community, who praise her for her dedication and sincerity, she reflects: "Being positive and refusing to accept defeat is a source of benefit. My determination to strive tenaciously day after day for kosen-rufu, united in spirit with my mentor, and to encourage as many young people as I can will never waver!"

Such great, unsung women are shining everywhere, their presence like the sun. That is why our movement for kosen-rufu is vibrant and strong.

Prof. Kevin Clements, chair in peace and conflict studies at New Zealand's University of Otago, has expressed profound admiration for the women's division members who have been making sincere contributions to help rebuild their devastated communities after the March 2011 earthquake and tsunami in Tohoku. *[On 14 March 2012, Professor Clements spoke at a seminar sponsored by the Soka Gakkai Women's Peace Committee in Tokyo. Prior to his lecture, two women's division members*

from areas affected by last year's disaster shared their stories of winning over adversity.]

The inspiring stories of women's division members taking the initiative to create positive value after the devastating earthquake and tsunami, he said, teach us the importance of hope in the face of adversity and the inherent strength and resilience of human beings. In particular, he noted, women play and have played a vital role in enabling human survival in the face of natural and man-made disasters throughout human history.[5]

The women of Soka are at the centre of efforts to build a peaceful, compassionate society that respects the dignity of life.

In offering encouragement to a women's division member, my mentor, second Soka Gakkai president Josei Toda, once said: "Chanting daimoku is a struggle to ignite the flame of courage in our life. You can definitely bring forth great benefit in the form of an astonishing positive transformation, changing poison into medicine. When you do so, your example will open the eyes of others to the power of the Mystic Law. You have an amazing mission in life!"

Let us all follow the example of our incomparable women's division members! By bravely chanting, striving and winning for kosen-rufu, let us present our honourable "mothers of kosen-rufu" with jewelled crowns of unsurpassed happiness!

You are smiling queens
who are always victorious,
surmounting
every sorrow
and suffering.

(*Value Creation*, June 2012, 7)

Notes:

1. May 3, Soka Gakkai Day, is also Soka Gakkai Mothers Day, in celebration of the women's division members, the "mothers of kosen-rufu".

2. Three obediences: Also, three submissions. A code of conduct derived from Brahmanism and Confucianism that required women to obey their parents in childhood, their husbands after marriage and their sons in old age.

3. Five obstacles: Also, five hindrances. Five obstructions to women's attainment of Buddhahood. The view that a woman cannot become a Brahma, a Shakra, a devil king, a wheel-turning king or a Buddha. This concept is referred to in a number of Buddhist writings and is mentioned and then refuted in the "Devadatta" (12th) chapter of the *Lotus Sutra*. This refutation takes place through the example of the dragon king's daughter who instantaneously attains Buddhahood, the most difficult of all five, when challenged by Shariputra on the grounds that women are subject to these five obstacles.

4. Osaka Rally: A Soka Gakkai rally held to protest the unjust detention of President Ikeda, then Soka Gakkai youth division chief of staff, by the Osaka District Prosecutor's Office in connection with the Osaka Incident. It was convened at the Nakanoshima Civic Hall in Osaka on 17 July 1957, the day of President Ikeda's release after two weeks of questioning by the authorities.

5. From article in *Seikyo Shimbun*, 25 March 2012.

Celebrating May 3, Soka Gakkai Mother's Day

Great mothers of Soka!
May you enjoy lives of happiness
   and peace.
All of you are noble Buddhas
striving for kosen-rufu.

O nce women get involved, they achieve the miracle of winning over everything,"[1] declared the Russian poet Marina Tsvetaeva (1892–1941). The strength, integrity and wisdom of women lead to victory.

Nichiren Daishonin writes: "Among all the teachings of the Buddha's lifetime, the Lotus Sutra is first, and . . . among the teachings of the Lotus Sutra, that of women attaining Buddhahood is first" ('The Sutra of True Requital', WND-1, 930). Women are an important focus of the Lotus Sutra, which teaches that all people have the potential to become Buddhas.

At the assembly where the Lotus Sutra was preached, the dragon king's daughter alone—cherishing the same spirit as the Buddha—actually demonstrated the principle of attaining Buddhahood in one's present form, which is the ultimate essence of faith in the Mystic Law. This was in stark contrast to Shakyamuni's leading male disciples, who only received prophecies from him of their attaining Buddhahood in future existences.

The sight of the dignified and resplendent form of the dragon king's daughter as a Buddha filled the hearts of Shakyamuni's bodhisattva disciples with great joy and unshakeable conviction in the power of the Mystic Law. They vowed to Shakyamuni to broadly teach the Law, undaunted by the three powerful enemies.[2] We could therefore say that a woman provided the initial impetus for victory in the struggle for the widespread propagation of the Law—in other words, kosen-rufu.

The women's division and young women's division together represent a gathering of "human flowers" (LSOC5, 142),[3] in complete accord with this legacy of the Lotus Sutra. The women's division, in particular, is the shining sun at the centre of the miraculous growth that has been achieved by the Soka Gakkai, which this year celebrates its 80th anniversary.

I am sure that founding presidents Tsunesaburo Makiguchi and Josei Toda would join me in giving a vigorous cheer for May 3, Soka Gakkai Mother's Day, filled with the deepest appreciation for the tireless efforts of our women's division members.

Mother!
Your devotion
moves us to tears.
May the heavenly deities
always safeguard and protect you.

Former United Nations Under-Secretary-General Anwarul K. Chowdhury praised women for working selflessly for the welfare of their children and families and society as a whole. Human society, he said, has flourished and survived because of this special characteristic of women.[4]

All humanity owes a profound debt to women and mothers. Having a sense of gratitude for them is the guiding light of a culture of peace. Nichiren Daishonin writes: "In order to repay my debt to my mother, I have vowed to enable all women to chant the daimoku of this sutra [i.e., Nam-myoho-renge-kyo]" ('The Sutra of True Requital', WND-1, 931).

The undertaking of "establishing the correct teaching for the peace of the land," set forth by the Daishonin, is the endless challenge of ridding the world of tragedies that inflict pain and suffering on mothers and children and instead creating peaceful societies that are radiant with their happy smiles.

The Daishonin continued to warmly encourage the lay nun Ueno, the mother of Nanjo Tokimitsu, who was mourning the loss of her husband and young son. In one letter to her, he writes: "One who embraces the Lotus Sutra will realize that hell is itself the Land of Tranquil Light" ('Hell is the Land of Tranquil Light', WND-1, 456). Through her steadfast faith, the lay nun Ueno paved the way to victory for her entire family.

The lotus flower blooms with unsullied purity from the midst of the muddy waters. We of the SGI are propagating the Mystic Law precisely so that mothers and indeed all those who have experienced great hardships and travails can attain unsurpassed happiness in life.

Mr. Toda said: "If you put faith first, you need never panic or get flustered. No matter what the problem or situation, the important thing is to chant about it deeply and strongly. Even when you feel deadlocked, that's precisely the time you can bring forth the true power of the Buddha."

> The benefit accumulated by
> our invincible mothers of kosen-rufu
> is vast beyond measure.

Praising the courageous faith of one of his female disciples [Nichigen-nyo, the wife of Shijo Kingo], who remained unshaken by great obstacles, the Daishonin writes: "You . . . are even firmer and more dedicated in your faith than I myself" ('On Rebuking Slander of the Law and Eradicating Sins', WND-1, 436).

On the evening of my inauguration as third Soka Gakkai president on May 3, 1960, a pioneering women's division leader from Kansai, who was a close relative of my wife, came to offer her congratulations at our home in Kobayashi-cho in Tokyo's Ota Ward. In greeting her, my wife said: "I regard today as a funeral in the Ikeda family," and "I've given my husband to the Soka Gakkai."

When the women's division members in Kansai learned of my wife's resolve, they were deeply moved. They vowed to unite with us and resolutely triumph in all struggles, while tirelessly striving alongside us to propagate the Mystic Law.

This vow to achieve continuous victory based on the shared commitment of mentor and disciple is the underlying spirit of Soka Gakkai Mother's Day.

Betty Williams, the Nobel laureate who made such an important contribution to peace in Northern Ireland, said: "One is a large number. If you can help one individual, one child, you will help ten. Because in the circle of that one person, there will be ten others that that one will educate."[5]

The courage of one woman can change everything. The expansion of the lively dialogues of our women's division members will give rise to countless waves of hope towards the creation of a peaceful and prosperous society through widely sharing with others the humanistic principles of Nichiren Daishonin's Buddhism.

Members of the men's division and youth division: While achieving your own great triumphs as well, please give a rousing cheer to the women's division, the noble mothers of kosen-rufu, to celebrate their brilliant victories for our movement!

> This is the era of
> our magnificent women's division,
> unrivalled anywhere in the world.
> May you continue your efforts
> to stir a fresh groundswell of kosen-rufu.

(*Value Creation*, May 2012, 7-11)

Notes:

1. Translated from Russian. Marina Tsvetaeva, *Sochineniya* (Works) (Moscow: Khudoz-hestvennaya Literatura, 1984), vol. 2, 11.

2. Three powerful enemies: Three types of arrogant people who persecute those who propagate the Lotus Sutra in the evil age after Shakyamuni Buddha's death, described in a 20-line verse section of the 'Encouraging Devotion' (13th) chapter of the Lotus Sutra. The Great Teacher Miao-lo (711–782) of China summarises them as arrogant lay people, arrogant priests and arrogant false sages.

3. *SGI Newsletter* Editors' Note: From 2010, all Lotus Sutra quotes will be taken from *The Lotus Sutra and Its Opening and Closing Sutras,* translated by Burton Watson (Tokyo: Soka Gakkai, 2009). Our citation will now read LSOC, followed by the chapter and page number. For a short period, we will continue including in brackets the corresponding chapter and page number in *The Lotus Sutra,* translated by Burton Watson (New York: Columbia University Press, 1993).

4. Translated from Japanese. Anwarul K. Chowdhury and Daisaku Ikeda, "Toward the Creation of a New Global Society" (tentative English translation), *Ushio,* June 2009 issue.

5. Comments made at a discussion session of the Hiroshima International Peace Summit, "Round Symposium: Think of Our Future," held in Hiroshima in 1 November 2006 <http://www. hiroshimasummit.jp/en/> (20 April 2010).

Essays

Lofty Emissaries of Kosen-rufu

A certain philosopher once said that just hearing the word "mother" produced a feeling of peace and comfort, warming the heart, and that if people gave more thought to mothers, there would be no war. I heard this profoundly moving statement as a youth, and I have never forgotten it.

The Russian writer Vladimir Korolenko (1853–1921) wrote that human beings exist to be happy just as birds exist to fly.[1] These are words worth pondering deeply. Human being or bird, each of us is here to fulfill our potential thanks in large part to our mothers who gave us life. That's why we must strive to build an age in which mothers' faces can beam with smiles of unsurpassed happiness and peace.

Exuberantly winning
victory after victory
for kosen-rufu—
Long live the women's division!
Long live their vibrant network!

Neither my wife nor I will ever forget the noble pioneering members of the women's division who earnestly took the lead for kosen-rufu day after day and created such magnificent history in the annals of our movement. The solid foundation that the Soka Gakkai enjoys today is the result of the "behaviour of Buddhas" demonstrated by these dedicated women's division members.

"I have a 'Japanese mother'—a member of the Soka Gakkai women's division." When French journalist Robert Guillain (1908–98) spoke these unexpected words to me, I leaned forward in anticipation. It was during our meeting in December 1974. For a total of close to 20 years, including during World War II and again in later years, Mr. Guillain was assigned to Japan as a foreign correspondent for the French wire service Agence Havas (later Agence France-Presse, or AFP) and the leading French daily *Le Monde*. The "Japanese mother" he referred to was the late Kuni Kanamori, who worked for him as a housekeeper. He affectionately called her "O-Kuni-san".

As a citizen of France, one of the Allied powers fighting against Japan, Mr. Guillain was under constant surveillance by the Japanese authorities during the war. His office was also searched. It was during this same period that Tsunesaburo Makiguchi and Josei Toda, the first and second presidents of the Soka Gakkai, were being harassed by the notorious Special Higher Police, known more commonly as the "thought police".

Mr. Guillain recalled fondly: "O-Kuni-san always warmly aided and supported me in those days when foreigners were persecuted by Japan's militarist authorities. She treated me as if I were her own son." When the military police came to his home to search for secret documents, O-Kuni-san staunchly protected him. Many years later, she reminisced of that time: "I might not have had much education, but I knew it was wrong to drag someone from another country into Japan's war, and I sincerely did my best to support and protect him." A mother's compassion, a woman's sense of justice, transcends national boundaries.

Even after returning home to France when the war ended, Mr. Guillain never forgot the kindness of his "Japanese mother". When he was posted in Japan for a second time in the late 1950s, O-Kuni-san also worked for him and his family. She had just joined the Soka Gakkai and started practising Nichiren Buddhism. And the third time Mr. Guillain was posted in Japan, in 1969, he and his family visited O-Kuni-san's home in Tokyo's Mitaka area to express their gratitude to her.

Mr. Guillain explained to me at our meeting: "I came to know about you, President Ikeda, through the example of pure and devoted Buddhist faith embodied by O-Kuni-san, and that's how I came to learn the truth about the Soka Gakkai." I was deeply moved to see how sincere, dedicated women like O-Kuni-san were serving as emissaries of the Soka Gakkai and spreading trust for our movement in society.

I invited O-Kuni-san, her daughter, and other members from her local area to attend the Soka Gakkai Headquarters Leaders Meeting held immediately following my encounter with Mr. Guillain. "I'll never forget you as long as I live," I said to her, shaking her hand. Tears of joy fell from her eyes as she said: "I'm so happy!" I still remember to this day her smile luminous with a deep satisfaction and fulfillment.

Throughout Japan and the world, countless noble women's division members just like O-Kuni-san, sharing my aims and spirit, are working tirelessly out of the limelight to staunchly protect the Gakkai and promote kosen-rufu. Even if we don't have the opportunity to meet them in person, my wife and I fervently chant daimoku for them every day.

Sir Yehudi Menuhin (1916–99), the world-renowned violinist and conductor with whom I shared an unforgettable encounter (in April 1992), wrote: "There is no flower without a root, and if it is to bloom it must be fed by something strong and steady."[2] And it is precisely because the women's division members are devotedly cultivating these invisible yet all-important roots that the Soka Gakkai blooms so luxuriously with the flowers of happiness, capable individuals, and victory.

Sir Yehudi, blessed with a superb natural musical gift, said that he was moved by the beautiful rhythm of Nam-myoho-renge-kyo and that he himself chanted it. Again, it was a women's division member—this time from the SGI-UK—who had taught him about Nam-myoho-renge-kyo.

The American civil rights activist Virginia Foster Durr (1903–99) declared: "The point is not how bad things are . . . the point is what to do about it".[3] What matters most is our heart, our spirit. Complaining gets us nowhere. Nothing is changed by tears and whining. Those who press forward with hope and joy no matter how daunting the challenges before them are true spiritual victors.

Durr also concluded: "The only way I see to remove prejudice is to be in association with people".[4] To open a new course, we must courageously reach out to and interact with others—in other words, engaging in heart-to-heart dialogue to foster ties of friendship and understanding.

In a letter to Nichigen-nyo, the wife of Shijo Kingo, the Daishonin writes: "You may call a stone a jewel, but that does not make it one. You may call a jewel a stone, but it remains a jewel. . . . People may slander the Lotus Sutra, but that does not affect it any more than calling a jewel a stone affects the jewel" ('The Gods Same Birth and Same Name', WND-1, 315). Whatever others may say to the contrary, the truth is the truth, and what's right is right. The important thing is to speak out loud and clear, without being afraid. As the ancient Roman philosopher Seneca asserts: "What madness it is to be afraid of disrepute in the judgment of the disreputable!"[5]

In any event, truly deep and lasting human ties are not created by the coercion of authority or by means of strategy; they are forged through personal courage, wisdom and integrity.

Our women's division members are lofty emissaries of happiness, peace and justice in the arena of grassroots diplomacy, surpassing all others.

Nobel Peace Prize laureate Betty Williams of Northern Ireland also treasures her interaction with Soka Gakkai women's division members. In the early years of her endeavours, Mrs. Williams said she struggled to find a balance between being a mother raising a family and a peace activist. She has said that her children once asked her why she left them at home to go out and work for peace.

There were many days when she felt too tired to go on and thought of giving up. But she refused to accept defeat, refused to abandon her struggle, no matter what anyone said. She was determined to change a society that held life so cheap. She was certain of her responsibility to create a peaceful society for the sake of her children's future. When she was told something was impossible, it only ignited her fighting spirit to prove them wrong.

Witnessing her tireless devotion to peace activism over the years, her children also eventually understood. When he was older, her son said to her: "I'm just beginning to realise, because of this situation in the world now, what you did when you were younger: you fought to save my life so that I wouldn't die."

Ms. Williams triumphed. And she has the greatest respect and trust for the women of the SGI, whom she regards as heroines of daily life.

Activities for kosen-rufu are a struggle to create a bright future 50 years, 100 years, 10,000 years hence. They are an impetus giving rise to a great tide of peace for endless generations to come. We are carrying out a proud and noble mission without compare.

Seneca also said: "I have looked upon every day as if it were my last."[6] This is very similar to the Daishonin's teaching of living with the spirit that now is the last moment of one's life.

On May 3 of this year—which was not only Soka Gakkai Day but also Soka Gakkai Mother's Day—a great pioneer of the women's division from Kyushu (the southernmost of Japan's four main islands) passed away peacefully.[7]

She joined the Soka Gakkai in April 1960, while in her final year of high school, and practised the Daishonin's Buddhism with unwavering dedication from her days as a young women's division member until the very end of her life. As a women's division member, she played an important leadership role in the Kyushu prefectures of Kumamoto, Kagoshima and her native Fukuoka, and indeed was active throughout the region. She had a fine family, and I knew them all well.

In the second half of April, she dictated her last will and testament to a family member from her sickbed. I'd like to share some passages with you.

I am overjoyed to have been able to share in a historic page of resounding victory together with my great mentor President Ikeda, Mrs. Ikeda, my beloved fellow members, and my dear family. Thank you all so much. . . .

I have lived with the sole desire of responding to Sensei's sincerity. I wish I could open my heart and show you everything in it. . . . All my life, when I was trying to help my friends with their problems, I would ask myself, "How would Sensei encourage them in this situation?" and when I faced my own problems, I would ask myself, "What would Sensei do?"

. . . It is my greatest joy that my three sons were all able to study at Soka University, the school Sensei founded. . . . My beloved husband, children, and grandchildren will carry on my determination to achieve kosen-rufu. I have no regrets in my life. . . . If you ever think of me, please exert yourself in my stead in expanding our circle of friendship and promoting understanding of the Gakkai. . . .

In the Daishonin's writings, there is the passage, "The sutra's statement, 'Those persons who had heard the Law dwelled here and there in various Buddha lands, constantly reborn in company with their teachers' [LSOC7, 178], cannot be false in any way" ('The Heritage of the Ultimate Law of Life', WND-1, 217).

I know that I will be reborn in the same world as President and
Mrs. Ikeda and continue our struggle.

As she was dictating these thoughts, she was wearing a beautiful
corsage, shining like a badge of honour. It was the corsage my wife
had worn at the April Headquarters Leaders Meeting and sent to her
as a gift.

Learning of her death, my wife and I placed our palms together
in prayer and chanted daimoku for the eternal happiness of this
great champion of kosen-rufu who had lived a life of complete
victory.

I once presented her family with these words:

When you're sad, I cry.
When you're happy, I leap for joy.
Sharing grief and sorrow,
let us continue battling
courageously together
throughout our lives.

The journey of the Soka family is one of eternity, happiness, true self
and purity together across the three existences of past, present and
future.

Florence Nightingale (1820–1910), the founder of modern nursing,
declared: "Progress is only a step to more progress."[8] These words
resonate with the ever-progressing spirit of Soka women, the belief
that not advancing is regressing.

The noted American writer and social activist Helen Keller (1880–1968), who overcame countless obstacles, vigorously asserted: "There is no royal road to the summit. . . . Every struggle is a victory."[9] Our women's division members have reached the summit of great victory in just this fashion, persevering tenaciously and taking one brave step forward after another.

The Brazilian astronomer Ronaldo Mourão, with whom I am presently conducting a dialogue, said fondly: "My mother taught me that you must never put off doing good for even a single moment. This was one of her most important legacies to me." This earnest, ever-present sense of purpose of mothers fosters capable individuals, changes the times, and opens a new page of history. It is the reality of human progress.

Why did Nichiren Daishonin propagate the Mystic Law in the midst of such harsh persecution? Solely to repay his debt of gratitude to his mother. In a letter addressed to the lay nun Sennichi, the wife of Abutsu-bo, he said:

> Since I have realized that only the Lotus Sutra teaches the attainment of Buddhahood by women, and that only the Lotus is the sutra of true requital for repaying the kindness of our mother, in order to repay my debt to my mother, I have vowed to enable all women to chant the daimoku of this sutra. ('The Sutra of True Requital', WND-1, 931)

World peace means a world in which mothers can be happy, in which women who lead their lives with seriousness and dedication day after day can attain the greatest happiness. The struggle to change the vector of human society in this way is the goal of kosen-rufu and the principle of establishing the correct teaching for the peace of the land (Jpn. *rissho ankoku*).

The French writer Romain Rolland (1866–1944) sternly warned: "It is unforgivable to fail to accord women the respect they deserve."[10] We must never forget that a shortcut to peace on all levels lies in political leaders everywhere implementing policies that offer the most reverent and sincere support to women of all classes.

Rise cheerfully
above the clamour,
and win through all.
The heavenly deities will protect you
as women of wisdom and philosophy.

(*Value Creation*, September 2007, 67-76)

Notes:

1. Translated from Russian. From a short story titled 'Paradox'.

2. Yehudi Menuhin and Curtis W. Davis, *The Music of Man* (Toronto: Methuen, 1979), 198.

3. Virginia Foster Durr, *Freedom Writer: Virginia Foster Durr, Letters from the Civil Rights Years*, edited by Patricia Sullivan (New York: Routledge, 2003), 416.

4. Ibid., 407.

5. Seneca, *Ad Lucilium, Epistulae Morales*, translated by Richard M. Gummere (London: William Heinemann Ltd., 1962), vol. 2, 445.

6. Ibid., vol. 3, 7.

7. Her name has been withheld out of respect for her family's privacy.

8. From a letter that Florence Nightingale wrote to the nursing staff and student nurses of the Nightingale Fund School at St. Thomas's Hospital, dated New Year's Day, 1886. (British Museum Archives).

9. Helen Keller, *The Story of My Life* (New York: Signet Classics, 2002), 75.

10. Translated from Japanese. Romain Rolland, 'Chari Bubia eno Tegami' (Letters to Charly Bouvier), in *Roman Roran Zenshu* (Collected Works of Romain Rolland), translated by Mitsuo Yamaguchi (Tokyo: Misuzu Shobo, 1983), vol. 38, 154.

The Victory of the Women's Division is the Victory of Soka

"O ne's body and mind at a single moment pervade the entire realm of phenomena" ('The Object of Devotion for Observing the Mind', WND-1, 366)—these are the immortal words of the Great Teacher Miao-lo of China. The inner realm of our life is so vast that it encompasses the entire universe.

When we chant Nam-myoho-renge-kyo with our whole being for the sake of kosen-rufu, we cannot fail to move the heavenly deities—the positive forces of the universe. As Nichiren Daishonin writes in a letter to a female follower: "If one can move Shakyamuni Buddha, the lord of teachings, can the grass and trees fail to respond, can the waters remain calm?" ('Letter of Petition from Yorimoto', WND-2, 811).

Similarly, when we speak to others based on earnest prayer, our words cannot fail to touch their lives. Let's therefore foster friendships with big, wide-open hearts. Let's courageously share our convictions and ideals with many others, cherishing each encounter. Every effort we make towards that end represents a brilliant opportunity to help others form a connection with Buddhism. Herein lies the path to creating peace. Herein lies the path to happiness and victory.

Serenely
live each day to the fullest,
reminding yourself,
"I am an expert in life!"
and let nothing cause you fear.

Three decades ago, on our fifth trip to China in April 1980, my wife and I were invited to the residence of Madame Deng Yingchao (1904–92) and the late Chinese premier Zhou Enlai (1898–1976) in Zhongnanhai in Beijing. A smiling Madame Deng greeted us warmly like a mother welcoming her children home after a long absence.

She showed us around the courtyard, sharing that it was only the third occasion that foreign guests had strolled along its paths and that she had long wanted us to see it. Crab apple blossoms, which were a favourite of Premier Zhou, were just beginning to bloom and lilacs, said to symbolise friendship, filled the inner garden with bright colour.

Madame Deng expressed her disappointment that, owing to her busy schedule, she had not been able to visit us at our home or see the Zhou Cherry Tree at Soka University during her trip to Japan the previous year (1979). When my wife presented her with an album containing photographs of the Zhou Cherry Tree, together with a fabric painting of the same tree by a young women's division member from Kamakura, her face lit up in delight. She described these gifts as a symbol of China-Japan friendship, past, present and future.

[SGI Newsletter *Editors' Note: The Zhou Cherry Tree was planted on the Soka University campus in Tokyo, on 2 November 1975, by President Ikeda and the university's six Chinese exchange students—the first Chinese government–financed exchange students to be accepted by a Japanese university since the establishment of the People's Republic of China. The tree was planted as an expression of their shared prayers for the health of the then ailing Premier Zhou and as a symbol of the wish for lasting peace and friendship between China and Japan.]*

Our conversation eventually turned to Madame Deng's marriage to Premier Zhou. Asking if I might pose a very Japanese question, I inquired if they had been brought together by a matchmaker. "I suppose if we had a matchmaker, then it was the May Fourth Movement,"[1] she replied, her voice filled with nostalgia.

When Madame Deng and Premier Zhou were young, they had stood up bravely and risked their lives to fight for their homeland. I was deeply struck by the fact that Madame Deng still referred to her late husband as "Comrade Enlai". Bound together as they were by their dedication to the people, marriage meant being comrades in a united cause. Even after her husband's death, Madame Deng remained true to their shared commitment.

In much the same way, my wife and I, following Josei Toda as our great mentor in life, have dedicated our lives to the grand adventure of kosen-rufu as comrades in a shared struggle.

The power of women, of wives and of mothers is truly awe-inspiring.

In praise of Toki Jonin's wife Myojo, who assisted and supported her husband, the Daishonin writes: "It is the power of the bow that determines the flight of the arrow . . . and the strength of the wife that guides the actions of her husband" ('The Bow and Arrow', WND-1, 656).

My wife and I had the good fortune of meeting with Madame Deng on eight separate occasions, starting in 1978. Madame Deng declared that when she made a true friend, she would cherish that friendship forever. And, indeed, she treated us with the utmost kindness and consideration throughout her life.

In May 1990, on our seventh trip to China, Madame Deng again invited us to her home. During that visit, I expressed my heartfelt wishes for the good health of this great and beloved mother of the Chinese people. As our visit came to a close and my wife and I were in the car about to leave, Madame Deng came all the way to the outer gate to see us off in spite of her advanced age. We immediately stepped out of the car and together bowed deeply to her once more. Then, as we left by car, we continued waving to her until we could no longer see her. My wife and I prayed with all our hearts that our dear friend would live many more long years.

Madame Deng was a wonderful person who gave her whole life to working for the welfare of the people.

She herself held a number of important government posts, but she was always friendly and forthright. Pretension and callousness were completely foreign to her nature. She deeply empathised with people's sufferings and actively took steps to find solutions to the problems they were facing.

Madame Deng once said to a fellow female leader: "Women have many things to worry about—their partners, their families, and countless other things. If women leaders forget the sufferings of their sisters and neglect women's problems, then just who will solve them?"[2]

Your proud
dedication to kosen-rufu
will fragrantly adorn your life
with infinite treasures
throughout the three existences.

In the Soka Gakkai, there are countless admirable women who exert themselves unsparingly for the happiness of others and the welfare of society. They do this while holding down jobs, doing household chores, raising children, and participating in their communities. They are extremely busy. But while taking care of personal or family responsibilities, they also encourage and support their friends and try to make the world a better place. What a marvellous example they are for others!

Once again this year, women's division members have sent me reports about the cherry blossoms at various Gakkai facilities across Japan. The first was about the trees at the Okinawa Peace Memorial Park in the south, which bloomed in January, while the last was about those at the Toda Memorial Park in Atsuta, Hokkaido, in the north, which finally bloomed in May.

Many community leaders attended the now annual cherry blossom viewing festival at the Atsuta memorial park, which has become one of Hokkaido's top scenic spots for cherry blossoms. I can picture the statue of Mr. Toda there, bathed in tranquil light, amid 8,000 cherry trees in glorious full bloom after weathering the long winter. It makes me very happy that the members and residents of Atsuta, Mr. Toda's beloved hometown, take great pride and joy in this park.

The Mother Cherry Tree at Sapporo Soka Kindergarten in Hokkaido has also bloomed again this year. When I visited the kindergarten in April 1976, I proposed that cherry trees be planted in honour of the children's mothers and fathers. Two saplings were then planted by representatives of the children's parents during my visit.

I know that mothers often make great financial sacrifices in order to be able to send their children to the Soka schools. The Mother Cherry Tree is a tribute to them, the true supporters of Soka education.

Another Mother Cherry Tree graces the Nishinari Culture Center in Osaka, in honour of my esteemed Kansai women's division members. This cherry tree also bloomed splendidly again this year, along with the Ichi Cherry Tree, which is named after my own mother [Ichi Ikeda], who had many memorable encounters with members in Kansai.

Yet another Mother Cherry Tree grows at the Shinano Culture Center (formerly, the Soka Women's Center), welcoming members from Japan and around the world together with the Youth Cherry Tree that stands in front of the Soka Gakkai Headquarters. In the spring-time, the Mother Cherry Tree brightens the hearts of all who see it. It is a symbol of our women's division members who play such a key role in fostering the youth division and opening the way to the future.

In a letter she sent to a friend while personally struggling amid great adversity, the antiwar activist Rosa Luxemburg (1870–1919) wrote in cheerful encouragement: "So, in any case: Chin up and don't lose heart!"[3]

The women's division members are all great, victorious "Mother Cherry Trees", forever standing tall, faces lifted to the sun, filled with self-confidence and imparting courage and hope to all around them.

Never be defeated,
never ever give in to defeat.
My friends,
that is the way to build
a triumphant citadel of happiness.

The Daishonin referred to the female follower Nichimyo as 'Sage Nichimyo', and the lay nun Konichi, as 'Honorable Konichi'. In those days, the titles "Sage" and "Honorable" were used to designate people who were as venerable or respectworthy as enlightened Buddhas or bodhisattvas. In the realm of Buddhism in 13th-century Japan, very few women, if any, received this distinction. The Daishonin's conferral of these titles on women followers, therefore, represents a profound departure from the generally prevalent attitude towards women at that time.

Neither Nichimyo nor the lay nun Konichi were from well-known or noble families. One was an ordinary woman striving on her own to support a young child, and the other a woman who had lost both her husband and beloved child. But with the Daishonin's encouragement, they were able to maintain strong faith and not be defeated by any obstacle or persecution they encountered.

You don't need social standing or fortunate material circumstances to help others or work for kosen-rufu. On the contrary, truly admirable are those who strive for the welfare of others and dedicate themselves to advancing kosen-rufu, even when facing the most daunting personal challenges. Such people are truly noble Buddhas. They will definitely be able to bring beautiful flowers of happiness to bloom for both themselves and others, wherever they are.

The women's division members are joyfully walking this supreme path of life imbued with eternity, happiness, true self and purity.

With a lofty nobility
as fragrant as white lilies,
the women of Soka are expanding
a network of peace and victory
around the world.

June 10, Women's Division Day, will soon be here. It has become a day when people across the globe express praise and gratitude for the women of Soka.

Dr. Sarah Wider, poet and former president of the Ralph Waldo Emerson Society in the United States, has expressed great admiration for the women's division's efforts to promote dialogue. She says: "When I wish to be hopeful, I think of the members of the Soka Gakkai women's division."[4]

The women of Soka are the conscience of the world! They are the sun of humanity! The noble women of Soka have a profound mission to bring a bright sense of hope for the future to those around them.

The Japanese poet Yoshiko Mikajima (1886–1927) wrote: "My sole concern is to keep challenging myself in every way possible,"[5] and "I call out in my heart, 'Be stronger!'"[6]

As the women of Soka who uphold the foremost philosophy of Nichiren Daishonin's Buddhism, please forge ahead cheerfully, with strength and confidence. Have an intrepid fighting spirit. Unhesitatingly speak out for what is right. And have courage. Where there is courage, the sun of hope and justice shines.

None are stronger or nobler than the women of Soka who summon forth "the heart of a lion king" ("Letter from Sado', WND-1, 302), through earnestly chanting Nam-myoho-renge-kyo, and engage others in dialogue based on their firm conviction in faith.

This is the way the Soka Gakkai has successfully advanced kosen-rufu and made progress in achieving the Daishonin's goal of "establishing the correct teaching for the peace of the land".

The difference between courage and cowardice is subtle. A fine line divides them. Often just a few words of encouragement can give us an enormous boost of energy and courage. The English word "encourage" literally means to "impart courage". Where there is warm encouragement, people brim with courage.

Having courage in all things, let's create a powerful solidarity and keep pressing forward confidently.

> Always and forever
> cherishing
> a youthful spirit,
> leave behind a brilliant legacy
> of your life in this world.

The underlying strength of our Soka movement resides in the vigour and unity of our dedicated members who press on unflaggingly, overcoming all difficulties no matter how challenging, to create a powerful momentum for our ongoing victory.

It was also in the spring month of May during the Osaka Campaign[7] of 1956 that Osaka Chapter achieved a historic record of introducing the Daishonin's Buddhism to 11,111 new member households in a single month, and neighboring Sakai Chapter, though still small by national standards, triumphantly accomplished a monthly total of 1,515 new member households.

The Gakkai's dynamic surge mirrored the line, "Our advance creating a sweeping momentum," from the Gakkai song "Ifu Dodo no Uta" (Song of Indomitable Dignity), which originated in Kyoto. As a result of this heroic campaign for kosen-rufu, beautiful flowers of dialogue bloomed throughout the entire Kansai area and led to the creation of many new friends and allies for the Soka Gakkai.

At the centre of this effort to promote dialogue were the women's division members, the mothers of Ever-victorious Kansai, who chanted wholeheartedly and strove their hardest with tremendous vigour, optimism, and energy. One such Kansai woman's division member later declared with deep emotion that this campaign was the very purpose for which she had been born.

The month of May then gave way to June—following the inexorable rhythm of the seasons that prompted the Daishonin to write: "Though we may wish for spring to linger, it must give way to summer" ('The Blessings of the Lotus Sutra', WND-1, 672). In that early-summer month of June, women from each area of Kansai packed the Nakanoshima Civic Hall in Osaka for a lively and invigorating women's division general meeting. I accompanied Mr. Toda to that gathering.

The mothers of kosen-rufu are strong, steadfast and never defeated. Their prayers are invincible.

Mr. Toda warmly said to the women gathered on that occasion: "In whatever form the three obstacles and four devils[8] might assail us, let's persevere in faith, support and help each other, and confidently continue day after day to build happy lives!"⁹

The victory of the women's division is the victory of Soka.

I am presently engaged in an ongoing dialogue via correspondence with Gao Zhanxiang, chairman of the Chinese Culture Promotion Society (CCPS) in China. [SGI Newsletter *Editor's Note: The dialogue, which began serialisation in the May 2010 issue of the Soka Gakkai–affiliated* Ushio *magazine, is titled 'The Unifying Power of Culture' (tentative English translation).*]

In April 1979, incidentally, Mr. Gao (as head of a delegation from the All-China Youth Federation) and I planted a pair of trees named the Zhou Enlai and Deng Yingchao Cherry Trees, in honour of the Chinese premier and his wife, on the campus of Soka University in Tokyo. The trees, which stand near the Zhou Cherry Tree planted four years earlier, are a further symbol of the deep ties of friendship between China and Japan.

In our dialogue, Mr. Gao has emphasised the significant role of culture and the importance of human harmony and solidarity: "Harmony creates beauty, and unity creates strength. The strength of unity is the strongest force for social progress and the development of the human race."¹⁰

Unity is strength. Genuine unity isn't perfunctory or the result of someone's clever manipulation. As the Daishonin says, "It is the heart that is important" ('The Strategy of the Lotus Sutra', WND-1, 1000). Indeed, the key to forging unity is sincerity that shines with integrity. Sincerity and integrity can create lifelong bonds of friendship and ultimately foster the best possible allies one can possess.

As Madame Deng called out to the younger generation: "Sincerity can pierce even metal and stone."[11]

Chant daimoku with wholehearted sincerity. Meet with members and support them with wholehearted sincerity. Even the most difficult circumstances and the most challenging human relationship problems can be solved with genuine goodwill and sincerity.

Twenty years ago (in 1990), Madame Deng not only presented me with a favorite jade pen stand of hers, but also a precious ivory paper knife that belonged to her husband. The paper knife, a token of her friendship and faith in me, shines more brightly than any gold.

Polishing our jewelled swords of faith so they too shine with unsurpassed brilliance, let us continue to tell others about our lofty cause with courage and confidence. Let's also continue to thoroughly polish our characters.

None are more resplendent than you, the members of the women's division, the noble mothers of kosen-rufu, whose very presence is like the sun. May you enjoy happiness and great victory! When the radiance of each one of you illuminates the lives of those around you, the great light of Soka will vanquish the darkness of these troubled times and shine brightly to celebrate our magnificent triumph.

Your lives are citadels
of brilliant triumph
that illuminate
your families
like the rising sun.

—Sincerely praying together with my wife for the health and happiness of our infinitely noble women's division members.

(*Value Creation*, August 2010, 24-38)

Notes:

1. May 4th Movement: An intellectual and social reform struggle that took place in China from 1917 through 1921, the pivotal event of which took place on 4 May 1919, in Beijing, China, from which the movement takes its name.

2. Translated from Japanese. From a dialogue between President Ikeda and Lin Liyun, who served as a Chinese-Japanese interpreter for Premier Zhou Enlai, featured in *Seikyo Shimbun*, 7 November 1999.

3. Translated from German. Rosa Luxemburg, *Briefe an Freunde* (Letters to Friends), compiled by Luise Kautsky and edited by Benedikt Kautsky (Frankfurt am Main: Athenäum Verlag, 1986), 115.

4. Translated from Japanese. Article in *Seikyo Shimbun*, 13 March 2010.

5. Translated from Japanese. Yoshiko Mikajima, *Mikajima Yoshiko Nikki* (Diaries of Yoshiko Mikajima), edited by Minami Kurakata (Tokyo: Shigei Shuppan-sha, 1981), vol. 1, 240.

6. Ibid., vol. 2, 574.

7. Osaka Campaign: In May 1956, the Kansai members, uniting around a young Daisaku Ikeda, who had been dispatched by second president Josei Toda to support them, introduced 11,111 households to the practice of the Daishonin's Buddhism. In elections held two months later, the Soka Gakkai–backed candidate in Kansai won a seat in the Upper House, an accomplishment that was thought all but impossible at the time.

8. Three obstacles and four devils: Various obstacles and hindrances to the practice of Buddhism. The three obstacles are (1) the obstacle of earthly desires, (2) the obstacle of karma, and (3) the obstacle of retribution. The four devils are (1) the hindrance of the earthly desires, (2) the hindrance of the five components, (3) the hindrance of death, and (4) the hindrance of the devil king.

9. Translated from Japanese. Josei Toda, *Toda Josei Zenshu* (Collected Writings of Josei Toda), (Tokyo: Seikyo Shimbun, 1984), vol. 4, 453.

10. Translated from Japanese. Daisaku Ikeda and Gao Zhanxiang, *Chikyu o Musubu Bunka-ryoku* (The Unifying Power of Culture), *Ushio,* May 2010 issue.

11. Translated from Japanese. Article in *Seikyo Shimbun,* 20 September 2003.

Women Paving the Way to a Century of Humanity—Part 1

Noble women,
eternal suns
from time without beginning,
enfold others
in your compassion.

A new sun has risen. This month (June) marks the 60th anniversary of the establishment of the Soka Gakkai women's division, a truly admirable network of women striving for peace and human happiness.

Nichiren Daishonin writes: "You will grow younger, and your good fortune will accumulate" ('The Unity of Husband and Wife', WND-1, 464). Our women's division members are advancing with unflagging youthful energy and brimming with ever-growing good fortune.

This month, women's division general meetings are being held throughout Japan and round the world. Each day, I receive reports from our women members conveying their joy and determination.

In areas hit by the March 11 Tohoku earthquake and tsunami, women's division members are gathering together and wholeheartedly encouraging one another, sharing their resolve to not be defeated and to overcome this terrible disaster.

My wife and I are chanting earnestly for everyone's happiness. Hearing of the members' valiant struggles, our hearts are filled with deep respect and admiration.

I recently received a report about a women's division meeting that was held at the University of Nairobi in Kenya and attended by many friends and distinguished guests. After two moving personal experiences in faith, a chorus sang the song "Mother" and a group of performers danced for the audience. This was followed by a speech on women's human rights in Africa by the eminent attorney Kaari Betty Murungi, who is an expert in international human rights law. Mrs. Murungi expressed high hopes for the grassroots activities of the SGI.

In countries across the globe, women who uphold the Mystic Law are creating and spreading tremendous joy as they strive to realise peace and happiness for all. The light of their joyous lives vibrantly illuminates their neighbourhoods, communities, towns, cities and society at large.

When the women's division was founded on 10 June 1951, President Toda composed this poem:

> A noble gathering
> Like fragrant white lilies
> Pure-hearted friends.

He cherished the women's division members, whom he regardedas noble and pure-hearted as beautiful white lilies.

In June 1956, 55 years ago, during the historic Osaka Campaign,[1] President Toda and I attended the Joint Osaka and Sakai Chapter Women's Division General Meeting held at the Nakanoshima Civic Hall in Osaka.On that occasion, Mr. Toda acknowledged that as Gakkai members, we would undoubtedly face a relentless onslaught of obstacles as we strove to promote the lofty cause of kosen-rufu. But he said: "No matter what hardshipswe may encounter, let us resolutely uphold faith and support one another as we strive unhesitatingly each day to build happy lives!"

Early on, my mentor lit the flame of the ever-victorious Kansai spirit in the hearts of the women's division members.

I also addressed the gathering that day, calling on those present: "Let's be genuine examples of faith so that we win the admiration of the people of Osaka, and let's conduct wonderful activities of which we can be truly proud!"

It was an unforgettable women's division meeting that my mentor and I attended together.

> Mother! Ah, mother!
> What a richly mysterious
> power you possess![1]

At the recent Nationwide Women's Division Leaders Meeting commemorating the division's 60th anniversary,[2] the young men's division Shinano Choir and the young women's division Fuji Chorus together performed a beautiful rendition of the song "Mother", as an expression of gratitude to all mothers. The women's division White Lily Chorus also gave a stirring performance of the Gakkai song "Ever in High Spirits" (the Japanese original of "Forever Sensei").

Our women's division members, the mothers of kosen-rufu, have advanced day after day, demonstrating the power to live on and remain undefeated. The great development of our Soka movement dedicated to realising the victory of the people is truly due to the "richly mysterious power" of mothers. Mothers, incredibly noble mothers of kosen-rufu, thank you!

I first presented my poem "Mother" in 1971, in commemoration of the women's division's 20th anniversary, at a Kansai women's division leaders meeting held in Osaka on 4 October. Five years later, in August 1976, the song "Mother", comprising excerpts of this poem, was completed.

To celebrate the women's division's 60th anniversary this year, a commemorative plaque featuring the lyrics of the song "Mother" was unveiled at the Soka International Women's Center in Shinanomachi, Tokyo (on 3 June 2011), bringing members fresh joy.

In April this year, our members in affected areas throughout Tohoku held their first discussion meetings since the March 11 earthquake and tsunami.

At a discussion meeting in Miyagi Prefecture, after members had shared their experiences and emotions following the disaster, a men's division leader took a small packet out of his bag. It contained a harmonica. Saying he would like to perform a tune as an expression of his profound appreciation for the women's division members, he began to play "Mother". He himself had always been encouraged by his own mother playing the harmonica. His performance enveloped the discussion meeting in a gentle and warm atmosphere. Some members moved their heads in time with the music, some hummed along, and some wept as he played on. Everyone's eyes brimmed with tears as they thought of the invincible spirit of mothers.

Louisa May Alcott (1832–88), the author of *Little Women,* wrote of her mother: "Life has been so hard for her and she so brave, so glad to spend herself for others. Now we must live for her."[3]

In a letter to the lay nun Sennichi, the Daishonin writes: "Now you should make a great vow and pray for your next life" ('Embankments of Faith', WND-1, 626). In this way, he encourages a follower who was striving hard in troubled times to help and support her fellow practitioners. Women's division members are confidently following the path set forth by the Daishonin, enabling themselves and others to realise a life-state of eternal happiness based on the great vow for kosen-rufu.

The prayers of mothers
resounding

through the heavens
are as deep as
the prayers of Buddhas.

The first of the five guidelines of the women's division is "Everything starts with prayer."

The members of the women's division chant earnestly each day. Their day begins with deep, determined prayer, and that determined prayer stays with them throughout the day. They chant powerfully and resolutely. They chant for their partners' health, for the growth of their children, for their families' happiness. They chant for the success and safety of members in their community. They chant for everyone's safety and protection, believing that having no accidents is victory. They chant for security and stability today and for peace tomorrow.

A youth recalled with tears in his eyes: "I'll never forget the sight of my mother constantly chanting."

There is no limit to the prayers of the mothers of kosen-rufu. There is no deadlock. These women are neither cowardly nor hesitant. Underneath their focused, steadfast prayers burns a courage that dispels all despair and resignation.

Prayer based on the Mystic Law means making a vow to be victorious. The moment we chant with deep prayer, our future victory is assured. It is to practice with our lives the "wonderful single Law that simultaneously possesses both cause and effect" ('The Entity of the Mystic Law', WND-1, 421).

The Daishonin promises:

Though one might point at the earth and miss it, though one might bind up the sky, though the tides might cease to ebb and flow and the sun rise in the west, it could never come about that the prayers of the practitioner of the Lotus Sutra would go unanswered. ('On Prayer', WND-1, 345)

This describes the prayers of the practitioners of the Lotus Sutra.

Our women's division members are champions of faith who have demonstrated, through the shared commitment of mentor and disciple, the tremendous beneficial power of the Mystic Law for achieving absolute victory. The beautiful blue planet on which we live, travelling ceaselessly through the universe, is enveloped in the daimoku of these great women.

I have expressed my vision for the 21st century in many different ways. I have called the 21st century the Century of Africa, the Century of Women, the Century of Human Rights, the Century of Dialogue, the Century of Education, and the Century of Life. Some people dismissed my ideas at first, but I have always sowed seeds of positive value for the sake of the future.

The Daishonin writes: "Even one seed, when planted, multiplies" ('Cloth for a Robe and an Unlined Robe', WND-2, 602). Basing my actions on prayer, I have sown many seeds and then nurtured and fostered them. This has been a challenging endeavour, but without such steady, painstaking efforts, the great tree of kosen-rufu would not have come into being.

Women's division members have joyously and courageously worked alongside me day after day to continue planting one seed after another and enable as many people as possible to forge a connection with Buddhism. No matter how they have been criticised or spoken ill of, they have never given up or faltered, persisting in their effort to plant seeds of hope, friendship, and peace in the earth of the people. Not only have they planted those seeds, but they have cultivated and nurtured their growth as well.

We have given our all to bringing flowers of positive value into bloom and helping people walk the path of happiness. Our movement for worldwide kosen-rufu has developed beyond anyone's expectations and we are making our dream of a 21st century of peace, culture, and education a reality.

As long as we have the sincerity, tenacity, wisdom and perseverance of the women of Soka—the mothers of kosen-rufu—the great flower of victory is certain to blossom for our movement. We will win through earnest dedication.

> Mothers of kosen-rufu,
> who sow the seeds of happiness—
> may you always
> dance with joy
> in every corner of the world.

(Value Creation, October 2011, 54-62)

Notes:

1. Lines from the song "Mother", the lyrics of which were composed by President Ikeda.

2. Held in conjunction with the 49th Soka Gakkai Headquarters Leaders Meeting at the Soka International Friendship Hall in Sendagaya, Tokyo, on 4 June 2011.

3. Louisa May Alcott, *The Journals of Louisa May Alcott*, edited by Joel Myerson and Daniel Shealy (Boston: Little, Brown and Company, 1989), 156.

Women Paving the Way to a Century of Humanity—Part 2

All Buddhas will surely protect
the noble mothers of Soka
who are joyfully working
to usher in
the dawn of kosen-rufu.

The Soka Gakkai will forever stand on the side of the people—
this is our fundamental spirit, which we have reaffirmed time and
again. This spirit is also manifested in our active commitment to value
and support mothers and women.

Mother! Our Mother!
Mother who has endured
the blizzards of fate,
forlornly imploring—[1]

There is a renowned German printmaker and lithographer Käthe Kollwitz (1867–1945), who was a contemporary of Soka Gakkai founding president Tsunesaburo Makiguchi. Kollwitz lost a son in the fighting during World War I and a grandson in World War II. Though she herself was persecuted in the last years of her life by the wartime Nazi German authorities, she boldly continued to produce her works of art.

Many of the works she created after her son's death depict mothers and children. There is a scene of a mother enfolding her child protectively in her arms and of a mother cradling her dead child. Another print depicts a tight huddle of women, arms wrapped around each other's shoulders, trying to protect their children, whose faces peer out from their midst. One of her most famous lithographs titled, "Seed Corn Must Not Be Ground" (1942), portrays a woman sheltering three small children in her solid arms.

The artist's own anguished cry emanates from these works. No doubt she wished that she could have protected her son and somehow prevented him from going to fight in a barbaric war. Her cry resonates with the fervent wish of all mothers who seek to protect their children, the seeds of the future.

"Sorrow shared brings people together,"[2] wrote Kollwitz. Empathy for others' suffering is the very foundation of women's solidarity in the cause of safeguarding life.

The Chinese author Lu Xun (1881–1936) also greatly admired Kollwitz, recognising that her creative work represented a struggle for human dignity waged through the power of a mother's love.

Kollwitz's prints and lithographs carry a powerful message for peace. In capturing the heartfelt cries of mothers everywhere, they unite people in the common desire for peace.

Almost two years after World War II ended, my mother finally learned that her eldest son—my brother Kiichi—had died in the fighting. Holding the death notice in her hand, she turned her back to us, her shoulders trembling as she quietly wept. I will never forget my mother's sorrow on that day. It seems to me now that in her silent mourning she was clasping her lost child in her embrace.

Mothers' love for their children is incredibly profound. We must adamantly oppose war and any other form of violence that causes pain and sorrow to mothers and robs children of their futures. World peace and the happiness for humanity all begin with treasuring and appreciating mothers—this is an unwavering conviction that I feel driven to stress and loudly proclaim for all to hear.

Today, in Germany, Japan, and all across the globe, SGI women's division members are energetically expanding their network for peace, and drawing widespread attention with their hope-filled activities.

In Mr. Makiguchi's copy of *The Record of the Orally Transmitted Teachings*—which was confiscated by the Special Higher Police during the war [but was returned to his family after his death]—the following passage is underlined: "While the word 'those' may refer either to men or women, here it is intended as praise for women in particular, and thus refers to women" (OTT, 185). This remark is made in relation to the Lotus Sutra quote: "If you can shield and guard those who accept and uphold the mere name of the Lotus Sutra, your merit will be immeasurable" (LSOC26, 352). The Daishonin thus declares that this Lotus Sutra passage especially praises women who uphold the Mystic Law.

I have solemnly engraved this passage in my heart, along with Mr. Makiguchi's spirit.

The influence of women was also very important in the American civil rights movement five decades ago, which sought to bring an end to racial discrimination and create greater social equity in the United States. Speaking of this movement, the American historian Vincent Harding, with whom I have published a dialogue, has observed: "It was very much a grassroots movement arising from local community organising . . . and, consequently, it is important to recognise that women really made up the heart of the movement."[3] Women were the driving force of the civil rights movement, he said, working patiently and persistently on the frontlines to talk with people and rally one person after another to the cause. Dr. Harding also voiced the view that without the practical, down-to-earth efforts of women, nobody would have come to attend the meetings or participate in the marches, and the movement would not have gone forward.[4]

Dr. Harding further emphasised that to create change, it is important for people of like mind to encourage one another and reaffirm the shared belief that success can be achieved. One concrete way of doing this, he suggests, is to share and listen to each other's experiences. Why? Because shared experiences establish a circle of encouragement in the community, he says, which then enables us to encourage people beyond the local community.[5]

There is deep significance in the way that Soka women, their activities firmly rooted in the local community, cheerfully and joyfully promote dialogue based on small gatherings or groups where participants can connect and talk with one another face-to-face.

Among the five guidelines of the women's division are "Cherishing our communities and societies" and "Joyfully sharing our experiences in faith."

Let us speak with voices brimming with hope and conviction! Let us take action with sincerity and consideration! In a cold and impersonal society where human connections are growing ever more tenuous, let us send forth the warm, uplifting sunlight of trust and respect. That is truly the noble work of the Buddha, enabling others to form a connection with the Daishonin's teaching and sowing the seeds for attaining enlightenment in their hearts.

Another of the five guidelines of the women's division is "Fostering young successors."

One month after becoming Soka Gakkai president, Mr. Toda established the women's division (on June 10), followed quickly by the young men's division and the young women's division (on July 11 and July 19, respectively). This was a truly inspired order of events, reflecting the fact that our women's division members play a vital role in fostering our young successors not only in the youth division, but also the future division [which was established later in 1964].

Last month (May 2011), Nara Chapter [in the Kansai Region] celebrated its 50th anniversary with a commemorative general meeting. I was happy to learn that 98-year-old Nobu Arima, the chapter's first women's division leader, also attended this meeting in good health and high spirits. The *Seikyo Shimbun* carried a photograph of her together with all the successive Nara Chapter women's division leaders on that occasion. Seeing it brought back many fond memories for my wife and me.

Mrs. Arima—a great pioneering member of our movement in Nara—took many young people under her wing and helped foster them into fine leaders for kosen-rufu. Incidentally, the new national young women's division leader, Yuki Yoshii, also hails from Nara. Mrs. Arima must be very proud of this.

Right after Nara Chapter was founded (in May 1961), someone covered the fence around Mrs. Arima's house with hateful anti-Gakkai graffiti. Mrs. Arima says she has kept the letter of encouragement that I sent her at that time. In it, I had cited a passage from the Daishonin's treatise 'On Repaying Debts of Gratitude,' in which he describes his own efforts to propagate the Law amid great hardship: "The difficulties I encountered became increasingly severe, like great waves that rise up in a gale" ('On Repaying Debts of Gratitude', WND-1, 727).

Even should dark storm clouds gather, as long as the women of Soka remain undaunted, a brilliant dawn of victory will never fail to come. Our past history has proved this.

The formula for the dynamic development of youth is the same round the world.

I have received a very inspiring report from India, where our organisation continues to grow at a remarkable pace. In one 53-member district in Kolkata, the women's division members—who made up the majority of the membership—resolved to create a more youthful organisation and set out to encourage and talk with young people around them. As a result, in just six months, they welcomed 21 new youth division members and 20 new future division members to their district.

The compassion of Soka women, who encourage and foster the youth, is the nurturing force that will ensure that the SGI remains eternally youthful.

The March 11 Tohoku tsunami flooded the second floor of the Soka Gakkai Kesennuma Community Center in Miyagi Prefecture. Fortunately, everyone taking refuge there escaped without serious injury. The area outside the centre was left strewn with wreckage and debris. A week after the disaster, a framed photograph was found completely undamaged inside the building. It was a photograph of cosmos flowers, the flower of the Tohoku women's division.

The name cosmos comes from the Greek word *kosmos* meaning "order" or "harmony". The flower is said to have been given this name because of its evenly spaced petals. This blossom reminds me of the beautiful hearts of the admirable people of Tohoku, who have astonished the world with their grace and orderliness in the face of a disaster that defies imagination.

Cosmos flowers, when blown down in a storm or gale, can put forth new roots from their fallen stems and grow vigorously again. They are surely the perfect emblem for our courageous Tohoku women's division members, who are battling bravely to overcome all adversity with the motto, "We will never bedefeated!" They are truly a fitting symbol of all the mothers of kosen-rufu, who have transformed their pain and sorrow into brilliant smiles of human victory.

The word *cosmos* is also a synonym for the universe, the starry heavens above. There is a cosmos within us (the microcosm of our life) and a cosmos outside us (the macrocosm of the universe). The life of each one of us is like a bright cosmos flower that blooms in wondrous rhythm with the law of the universe, the Mystic Law.

Moreover, the beautiful "flowers" of smiling mothers are a universal symbol of peace and happiness.

In a letter to the lay nun Sennichi, who lived on distant Sado Island, Nichiren Daishonin writes: "Though we live in the impure land, our hearts reside in the pure land of Eagle Peak. Merely seeing each other's face would in itself be insignificant. It is the heart that is important" ('The Drum at Gate of Thunder', WND-1, 949).

No matter how dark and troubled the times, we of the SGI who are dedicated to the Mystic Law and united in the beautiful and lofty spirit of mentor and disciple can continue to illuminate our families, communities and society at large with the inspiring light of hope.

The women's division members, connected by the most profound ties of shared purpose, are bringing flowers of happiness into splendid bloom wherever they are. And like the sun, a flower of the cosmos, they are lighting the way to a peaceful future for all humanity.

> Mother, may songs
> of dignity and peace
> be performed
> with your wisdom and philosophy
> on the surface of this planet
> that yearns for the arrival of spring.[6]

The wishes of mothers have never resonated as deeply in people's hearts as they do today. The voices of mothers have never imparted such courage to all as they do today.

Mothers of kosen-rufu, be strong! May all of you, our noble women's division members, enjoy happiness, peace, and good health.

I heartily applaud you, the great mothers of the century of humanity!

> Cherishing
> the unsurpassed jewel
> that nothing can destroy,
> adorn this existence
> with victory.

(*Value Creation*, October 2011, 62-71)

Notes:

1. Lines from the song "Mother", the lyrics of which were composed by President Ikeda.

2. Kaethe Kollwitz, *The Diary and Letters of Kaethe Kollwitz,* edited by Hans Kollwitz and translated by Richard and Clara Winston (Evanston, Illinois: Northwestern University Press, 1988), 65.

3. From the original English text of Dr. Vincent Harding's words in the dialogue, which appeared in the March 2011 issue of the Soka Gakkai–affiliated monthly magazine *Daisanbunmei* (The Third Civilization).

4. Ibid.

5. Translated from Japanese. Article in the *Seikyo Shimbun,* June 3, 2008.

6. Lines from the song "Mother", the lyrics of which were composed by President Ikda.

Suns of Happiness—The Women's Division Members—Part 1

"Shine! shine! shine!/ Pour down your warmth, great sun!"[1] wrote Walt Whitman (1819–92). He was a poet of the people who sang of humanity, life, and the universe. For me, these lines call to mind the women's division members, the noble mothers of Soka, who shine like radiant suns here on earth. They shine like suns in their families, in our movement for kosen-rufu and in society, and they warm frozen hearts with their bright compassion.

Whitman also wrote:"Oh, the mother's joys!/ The watching, the endurance, the precious love, the anguish, the patientlyyielded life."[2]

The mothers of kosen-rufu, our women's division members, too, are loving, strong, and incredibly dedicated.

Incidentally, Nichiren Daishonin gave many of his female followers Buddhist names that included the Chinese character for "sun" *(nichi)*— for instance, Nichimyo, Nichinyo, Nichigon, Konichi, and Onichi-nyo, among others.

And his famous words of encouragement, "Winter always turns to spring" ('Winter Always Turns into Spring', WND-1, 536), were written to a female follower [the lay nun Myoichi] who was facing many challenges [as a widowed mother].

I am reminded anew of the Daishonin's wish that women who embrace the Mystic Law would shine as invincible suns of hope, ushering in a springtime of happiness and victory in their lives without fail.

With great pride, let's salute the admirable women of the SGI, especially our women's division members, whose sunny presence is illuminating the world with the life-affirming philosophy of Nichiren Buddhism and paving the way to a new spring of peace for all humanity.

Knowing that you
are suns of victory
calling forth spring,
shine again today
with radiant smiles.

Although the first day of spring has passed according to the traditional lunar calendar, the chill of winter continues to linger in Japan. I wish to express my deepest gratitude to all our dedicated members who are delivering the *Seikyo Shimbun* newspaper each day in this cold weather, many braving slippery roads and sidewalks that are frozen or piled with snow. Each step they take on their rounds, as they deliver papers to one home after another, is a powerful driving force for the growth and development of our movement. Our newspaper deliverers are carrying out a noble "journey of faith" ('Letter to Niike', WND-1, 1027), just as the Daishonin describes.

My wife and I are always praying for the safety and health of all those who deliver the *Seikyo Shimbun* throughout Japan, especially those in the snowy northern parts of the country.

Nothing gives me greater joy than hearing about the great benefits and victories these uncrowned heroes have realised through their dedicated efforts for kosen-rufu.

In a letter to the lay nun Ueno, the mother of Nanjo Tokimitsu, the Daishonin writes: "One who, on hearing the teachings of the Lotus Sutra, makes even greater efforts in faith is a true seeker of the way" ('Hell is the Land of Tranquil Light', WND-1, 457). "Making even greater efforts"—this is the spirit of our women's division members, who continue to move forward intrepidly.

In my youth, I led a record-breaking campaign [the February Campaign of 1952] to introduce others to the Daishonin's Buddhism in Tokyo's Kamata Chapter. The enthusiastic efforts of the women's division members played a decisive role in our achieve-ment of an unprecedented 201 new member households in a single month.

The women's division members exerted themselves tirelessly to engage in one-on-one dialogue, each burning with courage and firm resolve to strive harder and further andto challenge themselves to talk to even one more person who was struggling or suffering. Because they gave their all by practicing in exact accord with the Daishonin's teachings, we were able to achieve a historic breakthrough in that February Campaign.

February 11 this year (2013) will mark the 50th anniversary of an essay I wrote, titled simply, "To the Women's Division". My mentor, second Soka Gakkai president Josei Toda, was thoroughly convinced that kosen-rufu would be achieved by women. I fondly remember picking up my pen on Mr. Toda's birthday (11 February 1963) to write this essay, with my mentor in my thoughts.

In a spirit of oneness with Mr. Toda, I called on the women's division members to always shine like the sun, to dauntlessly chant daimoku, no matter what storms of adversity might beset them, and to advance wisely to achieve victory in life. Responding to that call five decades ago, the women's division members throughout Japan stood up as "pilots of happiness" steering a sure course forward in their districts, chapters and families.

Even when they faced challenging problems such as illness, financial difficulties and family discord, they encouraged one another with the assurance that the scale of their karma was a reflection of the scale of their mission as well as the benefit they would eventually receive. And striving to elevate their life conditions "day by day and month after month" ('On Persecutions Befalling the Sage', WND-1, 997), they opened up new horizons for themselves and also helped positively transform their communities.

No matter what sufferings they might encounter, women who uphold the Mystic Law have the power to change any poison into medicine and become happy without fail. Our pioneering women's division members who belong to the many Treasures Group have accumulated countless such inspiring personal experiences. I am happy to say that their spirit is alive and well in their juniors, too, including the members of the young mother's group and the young women's division.

There is a women's division leader, whom my wife and I have known since she was in the high school division. She was born to a Korean father, who was brought forcibly to Japan prior to World War II, and a Japanese mother, who was a victim of the atomic bombing of Nagasaki. On both these counts, she experienced harsh discrimination from childhood. She also suffered from congenital health problems caused by her mother's radiation exposure.

In her teens, a friend, seeing her despair, strongly encouraged her to chant daimoku, saying it would revitalise her life. With a glimmer of hope that she might be able to change her situation, she decided to start practicing Nichiren Buddhism. Soon, she says, she felt tremendous joy and energy, as if she had been given a fresh lease on life.

Nichiren Daishonin says: "*Myo* means to revive, that is, to return to life" ('The Daimoku of the Lotus Sutra', WND-1, 149). With the great revitalising power of the Mystic Law filling her being, she threw herself into Soka Gakkai activities.

Later, she met and married a wonderful partner and, surmounting her health problems, gave birth to two children. Eventually, she moved to Yokohama in Kanagawa Prefecture—the place where President Toda delivered his Declaration for the Abolition of Nuclear Weapons. Because she had been through so much in her own life, she vowed to become a person who could understand the pain and suffering of others, and earnestly applied herself to expanding our network for peace in Kanagawa.

She recently reported to me that her daughter is earning top grades in a graduate programme at an eminent South Korean university.

This is one mother's story—an inspiring victory for human dignity and equality.

In my peace proposal commemorating SGI Day (January 26) this year, I outlined the following three guidelines for creating a world where respect for the dignity of life will prevail:

(1) The determination to share the joys and sufferings of others
(2) Faith in the limitless possibilities of life
(3) The vow to defend and celebrate diversity[3]

It is the positive, wise and broad-minded women of the SGI above all who are putting this into practice at the grassroots level.

This past 4 February marked the centennial of the birth of American civil rights pioneer Rosa Parks (1913–2005). I first met Mrs. Parks at the then Soka University Los Angeles (SULA) campus in Calabasas, California, 20 years ago (on 30 January 1993). I remember that we celebrated her upcoming 80th birthday on that occasion with a cake that my wife had organised.

Mrs. Parks, whose achievements as a noble champion of human rights shine in the annals of history, had a modest, pure and beautiful smile. Her determined, courageous words and actions in rejecting unjust racial discrimination, which had continued for far too long, famously started the wheels of history turning.

"I knew someone had to take the first step."[4] "Knowing what must be done does away with fear."[5] These are the immortal words of Mrs. Parks.

Nothing is stronger than a woman who acts on her convictions with firm resolve. No one can match her.

Speaking of the important contribution of women to the civil rights movement, the American historian Vincent Harding, with whom I have engaged in dialogue, said: "If women had not encouraged and inspired people to participate in the marches, there would have been no one to march."[6] He praised those women for their great "community organising power" and the fact that they "inspired people, strengthened them and guided them to participate" in the civil rights movement.[7] Just as Dr. Harding has repeatedly emphasised, at the heart of this people's movement that changed history was the encouragement of women.

The bright success of our movement for kosen-rufu has also been due to the unceasing encouragement of women. And the entire SGI will continue to achieve victory by members always warmly encouraging and supporting one another.

This 3 May will be the 25th Soka Gakkai Mothers Day, the day when we celebrate the noble mothers of kosen-rufu.

It is now 15 years since the title for women's division district leader was changed in Japan to better reflect their role as leaders contributing to the peace and security of their communities. [SGI Newsletter *Editors' Note: The English translation of the title remains the same.*] It is also the 35th anniversary of the start of women's division small study groups, where members gather together in small numbers for study and discussion.

Last month (January 2013), at the New Year's Headquarters Leaders Meeting, the motto for the women's division small study groups was announced: "Let's talk together, learn together and become experts in the art of happiness together!"

The small study groups of the women's division are places where members can get together to talk and to studyNichiren Buddhism in a more intimate setting than on the group or district levels. They are gatherings that most closely embody Mr. Toda's guideline that "Kosen-rufu begins with one-on-one, face-to-face dialogue."

Because of the small size of these study groups, everyone can play a central role, everyone can participate equally, irrespective of their position in the organisation. They are gatherings that allow everyone to join in together. This is the true strength of the women's division. Comprised of self-motivated women who warmly support and encourage one another, these study groups are the driving force for the development of kosen-rufu. With deep gratitude, let's applaud all the study group leaders and other women's division members who, with their sunny presence, are working ceaselessly to expand their network of smiling experts of happiness throughout the world.

> The castle of Soka
> resides in the pure hearts of
> women dedicated to kosen-rufu,
> eternally fragrant
> with treasures of happiness.

(*Value Creation,* June 2013, 61-71)

Notes:

1. Walt Whitman, "Out of the Cradle Endlessly Rocking", *Leaves of Grass* (New York: Dutton, 1968), 210.

2. Walt Whitman, "A Song of Joys", *Leaves of Grass* (New York: Dutton, 1968), 151.

3. See *SGI Newsletter* No. 8729.

4. Rosa Parks with Gregory J. Reed, *Quiet Strength: The Faith, the Hope, and the Heart of a Woman Who Changed a Nation* (Grand Rapids, Michigan: Zondervan Publishing House, 1994), 23.

5. Ibid., 17.

6. Translated from Japanese. Vincent Harding and Daisaku Ikeda, *Kibo no Kyoiku, Heiwa no Koshin* (Advancing for Peace through Hopeful Education), (Tokyo: Daisanbunmei-sha, 2013), 363.

7. Ibid., 364.

Suns of Happiness—The Women's Division Members—Part 2

The future of women
who are opening the way
to a glorious age of
worldwide kosen-rufu
shines with boundless hope.

Worldwide kosen-rufu—the widespread propagation of the Mystic Law throughout the entire globe—was the cherished wish of both Shakyamuni and Nichiren Daishonin. How infinitely profound, therefore, are the karmic ties we share as SGI members— united on the path of mentor and disciple—striving to fulfill this lofty goal at this significant time.

January 26, SGI Day, is also Tohoku Women's Day in the Soka Gakkai, a day on which we celebrate the wonderful women who are spreading hope radiant with the light of happiness in northeastern Japan. January

25, meanwhile, is Kansai Women's Division Day, a day that shines with the pride of champions of truth and justice.

In commemoration of SGI Day this year, representatives of our SGI translators and editors, who serve as a crucial bridge in the effort for worldwide kosen-rufu, presented me with a copy of a book by Helen Keller (1880–1968), *Teacher Anne Sullivan Macy,* along with a collection of excerpts from it, which they had translated into Japanese.

In the field of translation and interpreting, too, which is a lifeline for worldwide kosen-rufu, we find many dedicated women who are making tireless efforts to study and polish their skills. They have a mission of ever-growing importance.

Triumphing over the triple disability of being blind, deaf, and unable to speak, through the selfless instruction and training of Anne Sullivan (1866–1936), Helen Keller wrote with deep gratitude for her teacher: "She did not suit her actions to my weakness. She coaxed my spiritual faculties up to them."[1] These are words of profound meaning.

From childhood, Anne Sullivan had also experienced many hardships and struggles, including a battle with blindness [that ended in a successful operation that partially restored her vision].

To not only empathise with others and the sufferings they are going through, but to help them tap the boundless strength within them and to strive together for inner development— this is also the spirit of our women's division members who encourage and support others in carrying out their human revolution.

Looking back on her tutelage by Anne Sullivan, Helen Keller wrote: "I think that at that time Teacher [Anne Sullivan] felt like the roots toiling in the dark and cold to build up the delicate tissues of flowers, and it is a lovely recollection to me that she used to declare that this period of her life was the one most filled with delight and satisfaction."[2]

How noble is the challenging task of fostering others and how profound the joy one experiences as a result! To pray, rack one's brains, and take action for the happiness of our children, fellow members, and friends—such unseen efforts are certain to manifest in our own lives as wonderful good fortune and benefit. And that good fortune and benefit will also flow onto our children, fellow members, and friends.

In *The Record of the Orally Transmitted Teachings,* Nichiren Daishonin says joy means both oneself and others possessing wisdom and compassion (cf. OTT, 146). The women of the SGI, above all, are bringing flowers of unsurpassed wisdom, compassion and joy to bloom in their communities and the world. They are striving tirelessly for the great goal of kosen-rufu, working together in the beautiful unity of "many in body, one in mind". No one is stronger or brighter than they are.

The Soka Gakkai's first president and founder of Soka education Tsunesaburo Makiguchi, incidentally, was an early advocate of correspondence courses for the education of women. He was undoubtedly motivated by the firm belief that greater participation by women in society would contribute positively to the happiness and peace of all humanity. His spirit matched that of Nichiren Daishonin, who states: "There should be no discrimination between men or women" (cf. 'The True Aspect of All Phenomena', WND-1, 385), and "Women, *myo* [the mystic truth], and Shakyamuni are identical" (GZ, 842).[3]

But the situation of women in Japan today is still far from ideal. In the 2012 Global Gender Gap Report published by the World Economic Forum, Japan ranked 101 out of 135 countries— unfortunately, far below other industrialised nations.

The Austrian thinker Count Richard Coudenhove-Kalergi (1894–1972), with whom I published a dialogue, observed: "Women are far more dedicated pacifists than men. Endowed with an instinct for nurturing life, they abhor war and killing. In this respect, nature has given women a unique mission. . . ."[4]

When women shine, their communities, society and the future shine as well. I wish to assert once again that the way to peace lies in striving to realise a society where women can shine their brightest.

The women's division members of the SGI are pioneers in blazing that trail, and they deserve everyone's highest respect and trust.

January 17 this year marked the 18th anniversary of the 1995 Great Hanshin Earthquake [that devastated the city of Kobe in Hyogo Prefecture and surrounding areas in the Kansai region]. I offered sincere prayers in memory of all those who lost their lives in that disaster.

I am filled with the deepest gratitude and respect for the noble, ongoing efforts of our women's division members in Mighty Kansai who, with the determination never to be defeated, have devoted themselves to the task of reconstruction and revived their communities like phoenixes rising from the ashes.

Recently, my wife and I were deeply moved by the experience of a district women's division leader in Hyogo Prefecture, which appearedin the *Seikyo Shimbun* special feature page, "Fukko Shimbun" (Light of Happiness News). Though her husband and two daughters were killed in the earthquake 18 years ago, this admirable woman remained steadfast in her Buddhist practice and continued to exert herself tirelessly for the sake of kosen-rufu. I was also touched by the profound compassion of the senior in faith, who roused her out of her sorrow and self-pity with strict encouragement [as was shared in the experience].

The empathetic spirit of the Buddha—the spirit to share others' sufferings and sorrows and to pray with them for their happiness is the heart of Buddhist compassion.

While enduring all manner of slander and abuse, like that described in the Lotus Sutra, we have built the SGI, our great organisation for kosen-rufu, by reaching out to the friends and fellow members right in front of us who are struggling and suffering, offering them support and encouragement and illuminating even the darkest despair with the light of hope. It is an amazing organisation of the people without compare in the world today.

A young mother living in Miyagi Prefecture lost her beloved five-year-old son in the devastating earthquake and tsunami that struck the Tohoku region in March 2011. She was racked with unassuageable grief. She tried to respond to the warm support and encouragement of friends and family, but found it difficult to get back on her feet. What eventually rekindled hope in her heart was her correspondence with the district women's division leader in Hyogo Prefecture, whom I mentioned earlier and other Kansai women's division members [who lost loved ones in the Great Hanshin Earthquake].

For the past 18 years, these women of Ever-victorious Kansai have bravely forged ahead based on the Mystic Law, rising above the most painful sorrow.

Inspired by their indomitable example, the young woman from Miyagi has found the courage to carry on with her life. I have heard that she is now working hardas a Young Mothers Group leader in her local area, fortified by the belief that she is living and striving together with her son, who remains alive in her heart.

"It could never happen that a woman who chants Nam-myoho-renge-kyo would fail to be reunited with her beloved child" ('The Gift of Clear Sake', WND-1, 1092). The Daishonin wrote these words to the lay nun Ueno [the mother of Nanjo Tokimitsu], sharing in her grief and sadness on the death of her 16-year-old son [Shichiro Goro]. He continued to encourage her until the flame of faith burned even more brightly in her heart—a flame that was then inherited by her other son, Nanjo Tokimitsu, who also remained true and steadfast in his faith all his life.

Buddhism teaches the oneness of life and death. Our deceased loved ones are always with us in our hearts. They are united with us, never separate from us for an instant. Therefore, by making our lives brim with the power of the Mystic Law and taking action for the sake of Buddhism, for the happiness of others and for the realisation of kosen-rufu, we can brightly illuminate the lives of our departed loved ones and infuse them with "the greatest of all joys" (OTT, 212).

In any event, our sincere efforts to encourage and support others are sure to set in motion an unending chain of inspiring dramas of revitalisation. This is the realm of Soka.

The Daishonin clearly states: "All phenomena that exist are manifestations of the Buddhist Law" (WND-2, 844). Neither human revolution nor attaining Buddhahood in this lifetime happen separate from the reality of our daily lives, beset as they are by all manner of troubles and challenges. There may be times when we're tempted to complain, "Why me?" But it is by chanting and working to overcome our problems that we are able to manifest the power of the Buddha in our lives. Just as lotus flowers bloom beautifully in muddy ponds, the greater the hardships and challenges we face in our lives, the more splendid the flowers of victory we can bring forth through the power of the Mystic Law.

I am reminded of some words of encouragement that the Daishonin sent to the lay nun Toki: "[Your husband] hastold me that, while grieved at his mother's death, he was grateful that she passed away peacefully, and that you gave her such attentive care. He said joyfully that he would never be able to forget this in any lifetime to come" ('The Bow and Arrow', WND-1, 656). While struggling with her own illness, the lay nun Toki had nursed her mother-in-law, who was in her 90s. Fully aware of her efforts, the Daishonin thoughtfully conveys to her the gratitude her husband had expressed for this.

I have no doubt that the Daishonin is applauding the tremendous daily efforts of all of you, our women's division members. Therefore, whatever challenges you may face, I hope you will take them to the Gohonzon and calmly chant about them, not letting them control your life. By doing so, a way forward will definitely open up before you. In addition, your valuable experiences of triumphing over hardships through faith will in turn become a source of hope and inspiration formany others, especially the youth.

I would like to present the women's division members with some lines from a poem that the American futurist Hazel Henderson composed for her mother:

> This is true courage:
> To toil each day for others.
> This is true valor:
> To keep faith with the future,
> Without compensation or recognition.[5]

Now is the time to create the future. With the flame of faith burning ever brighter in your hearts, please boldly and courageously continue to make the most of each day, each month, and each year!

Together with you, the noble women of Soka, I will chant for the renewed development of our ever-victorious movement for kosen-rufu and impart warm encouragement for everyone's happiness and victory, in order to establish a solid foundation for the Soka Gakkai's centennial (in 2030).

Three cheers for our women's division members, who shine as bright suns of happiness and illuminate the world day after day!

Together, let's transform all hardships into a source of joy, and lead positive lives of unending victory.

> How strong and vibrant
> are your lives
> imbued with
> the immeasurable and boundless
> benefit of the Mystic Law!

(Value Creation, June 2013, 71-80)

Notes:

1. Helen Keller, *Teacher Anne Sullivan Macy: A Tribute by the Foster-child of Her Mind* (Garden City, New York: Doubleday and Company, Inc., 1955), 201.

2. Ibid., 51.

3. *'Oko Kikigaki'* (The Recorded Lectures); not included in WND, vols. 1 and 2.

4. Translated from Japanese. Richard Coudenhove-Kalergi and Daisaku Ikeda, *Bunmei: Nishi to Higashi* (Civilization: East and West), in *Ikeda Daisaku Zenshu* (The Collected Writings of Daisaku Ikeda), (Tokyo: Seikyo Shimbun-sha, 2003), vol. 102, 171.

5. Hazel Henderson and Daisaku Ikeda, *Planetary Citizenship: Your Values, Beliefs, and Actions Can Shape a Sustainable World* (Santa Monica: Middleway Press, 2004), 134.

Our Wonderful Network of Soka Women

We will fulfill our mission.
Come join us in the eternal citadel
in lifetime after lifetime,
and bring the cherry blossoms of youth
to bloom in beautiful profusion.

These are lines from the Soka Gakkai young women's division song "Cherry Blossoms of Youth", which debuted at the Tachikawa Culture Center in Tokyo, on 6 March 1978. It is a buoyant, uplifting song celebrating the lives of young women who dedicate themselves to the supremely noble mission of kosen-rufu.

Around the time when this song was unveiled, self-serving members of the Nichiren Shoshu priesthood and treacherous former Soka Gakkai leaders were secretly conspiring together against our organisation. In contrast, how pure and strong in faith were our young women's division members!

When the new song was being written, I offered several suggestions for both the music and lyrics, wishing to respond to the young women's sincere dedication. The completed "Cherry Blossoms of Youth" became a musical tribute to the indestructible bonds of mentor and disciple.

I firmly believed that as long as our young women's division members continued to raise their voices in joyous song, our movement would develop without end.

Today, 35 years since the "Cherry Blossoms of Youth" was first performed, the young women of that time have developed into outstanding leaders who, with unwavering commitment to kosen-rufu, are active on the front lines of their communities and society. Their lives shine with good fortune and wisdom. Keeping the cherry blossoms of youth blooming vibrantly in their hearts, they are also extending their care and encouragement to their successors in the young women's division as if they were their own sisters or daughters. This brings me immense joy.

A plaque inscribed with the lyrics to "Cherry Blossoms of Youth" adorns the lobby of the Soka Young Women's Center in Shinanomachi, Tokyo.

The spirit of ardently devoting oneself to kosen-rufu lives on in the hearts of our young women's division members round the world.

June 4 is the Day of the SGI Ikeda Kayo-kai. On this date four years ago (in 2009), my wife and I visited the newly opened Soka Young Women's Center in Tokyo for the first time, and participated in a commemorative gathering with women's division and young women's division representatives there. At that time, I presented the young women's division with five eternal guidelines.

Life is a struggle. When all is said and done, it is actually a struggle with ourselves. Will we triumph over our weaknesses or not? That is what determines our happiness or unhappiness. That's why, no matter what difficulties or karma we may be confronted with, we must never allow ourselves to be defeated.

We uphold the sound life philosophy of Nichiren Buddhism in order to build a strong, invincible self. The purpose of practising Buddhism in one's youth is to win over all obstacles and savour unsurpassed happiness in life.

I would like all of our young women's division members without exception to freely write their own unique story of happiness and victory as the most radiant and refined entities of the Mystic Law.

I spoke about these things on that day four years ago, in a friendly, family-like atmosphere.

I still remember the young women's division members beautifully singing "The Vow of the Ikeda Kayo-kai" that day.

With each passing year, the network of our young women's division members, the suns of happiness, continues to grow and shine ever more brightly.

This year again, I have received reports of cheerful and lively Kayo-kai gatherings being held across the globe [to commemorate SGI Ikeda Kayo-kai Day].

Nichiren Daishonin writes to a female follower: "As a woman you have inherited the life of the Lotus Sutra. In fact, you have inherited the life of the parents of Shakyamuni, Many Treasures, and the Buddhas of the ten directions. Is there anyone else in the entire land of Jampudvipa [the entire world] who possesses such good fortune?" ('The Entrustment and Other Chapters', WND-1, 916). He is saying here that women who embrace faith in the Mystic Law inherit the supreme wellspring of life—namely, Nam-myoho-renge-kyo— that is the source of all Buddhas.

In the muddy swamp of society, the young women's division members make their lives shine like beautiful lotus blossoms, imparting hope and inspiration. They are incredibly busy and may encounter many challenges. But that is precisely why they are able to accumulate boundless treasures of the heart day after day and enjoy lives of the greatest benefit in the world.

Umeko Tsuda (1864–1929) was a pioneer of women's education in Japan [founding the Joshi Eigaku Juku (Women's English School; forerunner of today's Tsuda College, a leading Japanese women's college)]. In the late 19th-century, a time of great change in Japan, Tsuda declared: "Women must have their rights regarded and be an influence for good in society."[1]

Women play such an important role in fostering life, protecting their families, supporting society, and illuminating the world. Groups and organisations that respect women's opinions and make good use of their wisdom will prosper and flourish limitlessly.

First Soka Gakkai president and founder of Soka education, Tsunesaburo Makiguchi, was also inspired by the strength and potential of women. That is why, as a young educator, he established a correspondence school for women.

June 6, Mr. Makiguchi's birthday, is also celebrated as Kanto Region[2] Women's Division Day. The women's division members of Kanto Region are solidly united and working energetically for kosen-rufu.

June 10, meanwhile, is Soka Gakkai Women's Division Day. On that day in 1951, the women's division was inaugurated and its members launched powerfully into action alongside second Soka Gakkai president Josei Toda. Mr. Toda said to those gathered: "I want you to know that women who uphold the Mystic Law are the most noble and praiseworthy of all. Please continue to strive together with me so that in the future we can show others what wonderful actual proof we have achieved through practising the Mystic Law."

In 1951, the Korean War (1950–53) was raging. At the women's division inaugural meeting, a member who originally hailed from Pusan (now Busan), Korea, expressed her firm resolve to dedicate her life to kosen-rufu and shared her wish for the peace of her homeland and the happiness of her fellow Koreans.

Sixty-two years have passed since then. Today, in South Korea, the exemplary civic-minded contributions of women's division and young women's division members have created a great flowering of friendship and trust in their communities and society.

One of the Daishonin's female followers, Nichimyo (also known as the mother of Oto), visited the Daishonin during his exile on Sado Island. She had separated from her husband and was raising her young daughter, Oto, on her own.

The Daishonin sent these words of encouragement to this sincere follower, which are no doubt wellknown to many of you: "In battles soldiers regard the general as their soul. If the general were to lose heart, his soldiers would become cowards" ('The Supremacy of the Law', WND-1, 613); and "The stronger one's faith, the greater the protection of the gods" (WND-1, 614).

Some of you might have thought these words were addressed to a male follower. They are indeed strong and bracing words. The Daishonin, however, had the highest respect for the tremendous strength of women. He even bestowed the honorary title "Sage Nichimyo" on this intrepid woman. And, as we see, he expressed absolute confidence in her as a "general", or great leader, in the struggle for kosen-rufu.

In these passages, the Daishonin seems to be calling out: "Observe my admirable and courageous female disciple!" "Heavenly deities, please praise and protect this dedicated practitioner and her daughter!"

I regard the Daishonin's aforementioned words of encouragement to Nichimyo as expression of his will and decree as the Buddha of the Latter Day of the Law to resolutely protect and support all SGI women's division and young women's division members.

The other day, my wife read a letter to me from a member in Yokohama, Kanagawa Prefecture,where she attended a women's division general meeting held on 27 May 1979, a few short weeks after I stepped down as third Soka Gakkai president.The woman, a greater block women's division leader (present-day district women's division leader) at the time, had welcomed my wife to the meeting with utmost sincerity.

In their discussion, my wife and the other women present agreed that as long as they continued practising with the Soka Gakkai no matter what, they were certain to become happy. This women's leader, too, has striven wholeheartedly for kosen-rufu over the past three decades with this unwavering spirit.

Not a single member present that day quit the Soka Gakkai. They all remained active and continued to receive wonderful benefits. Though some have passed away—including the woman's husband who, incidentally, served as the photographer for the meeting—their remaining family members have inherited their spirit in faith and are admirably working for kosen-rufu. While forging ties of friendship in their communities, each of them has demonstrated proof of the happiness that comes from living out one's life together with the Soka Gakkai.

The woman also reported that she continues to work on the front lines of our movement, actively reaching out to others in dialogue to promote kosen-rufu and achieve victory for the entire Soka family.

The Soka Gakkai shines with the achievements of such great individuals who have taken responsibility for the happiness of their communities, with the wish to transform them into true realms of joy.

The Daishonin also wrote this famous passage to Nichimyo: "Blue dye comes from indigo, but when something is repeatedly dyed in it, the color is better than that of the indigo plant" ('The Supermacy of the Law', WND-1, 615).

For the sake of and together with our wonderful network of Soka women, let us strengthen our faith even more, in the spirit of "becoming bluer than the indigo", and resolutely achieve victory in our efforts to create a peaceful world through spreading the humanistic ideals of Nichiren Buddhism.

The invincible prayers of women
allow them to take on difficult challenges
year after year
and transform their environment
into a bright realm of happiness.

(*Value Creation*, September 2013, 22-30)

Notes:

1. Cf. Umeko Tsuda, 'The Education of Japanese Women', *The Writings of Umeko Tsuda*, edited by Yoshiko Furuki, et al. (Tokyo: Tsuda College, 1984), 21.

2. In the Soka Gakkai organisation, the Kanto Region is comprised of Gunma, Ibaraki, Tochigi, Saitama and Chiba prefectures.

The Peerless Women of Soka—Part 1

I am fond of these words by the eminent Russian author Leo Tolstoy: "To polish oneself is more important than any other goal in life."

The women's division members of SGI truly shine as exemplars of such self-development; they lead profoundly meaningful lives that are a model of manifesting Buddhism in daily life.

A few days ago, a luminous full moon adorned the sky as the cloak of night solemnly descended. The moon's bright light reminded me of the smiling faces of our women's division members, the mothers of Soka. It was inexpressibly beautiful.

Kosen-rufu is an epic journey to realise world peace. Ignorant individuals criticise us, unaware of our lofty endeavour, while those consumed with angry resentment and jealousy sneer at our noble struggle for the sake of the Law, a struggle that will determine the future of humankind. Yet, they themselves do not lift a finger to benefit others or build a better world and, as such, never run the risk of incurring the inevitable criticism or derision that hounds those who champion good.

The true picture of kosen-rufu is that of a great movement dedicated to creating an era where all people win, where every last person can fully savour peace and happiness. That is the meaning of kosen-rufu.

Noble mothers of kosen-rufu—in winter, you walk through freezing, desolate streets to encourage friends and spread the teachings of Buddhism. Valiant mothers of kosen-rufu—in summer, you set off into the scorching, energy-sapping heat out of your concern for the happiness and welfare of others.

You embody the quintessence of humanity, dedicated as you are to helping people find a more real and solid happiness than any that might be found through reading countless books on the subject.

The unheralded emissaries of the Buddha who, exhausted at the day's end, make their way home silently and unseen, deserve greater recognition and admiration than any famous politician or celebrity. An American educator voiced this sentiment with tears in his eyes.

Today, our movement receives such praise and recognition from people all around the globe.

How wonderful is the sight of a mother walking hand in hand with her child as she advances happily along the path of her mission, or a mother who tenaciously presses onward, bathed in sweat, as she carries her tired, crying baby on her back.

All of your efforts are for the sake of others' happiness, for the Law, for peace and for your own victory.

Mothers of kosen-rufu—how admirably you exert yourself in society, where darkness and uncertainty reign, illuminating all with the light of your compassion.

Sublime mothers! Magnificent mothers!

You possess a heart of gold. With no thought of seeking personal recognition, you will give your all today and again tomorrow to encouraging those who are weighed down by heavy tears, helping them realise a state of happiness and a liberating lightness of heart.

Your spirit of selfless devotion will give rise to beautiful and unmistakable benefits that will last for a thousand years, ten thousand years and all eternity.

The American poet Joaquin Miller (1837–1913) wrote a poem titled 'Motherhood', which contains these lines that have always stayed with me:

> The bravest battle that ever was fought!
> Shall I tell you where and when?
> On the maps of the world you will find it not;
> 'Twas fought by the mothers of men.

Though your attire may be simple and modest, you wear in your heart a treasure that surpasses those of the wealthiest millionaire, your life radiating with an inexpressibly vibrant, golden brilliance.

When it comes to talking about Buddhism, you are prepared to take on anyone, be they prominent public figures or academics. You deftly repudiate and rebut shallow criticism and offer persuasive counter arguments. Such is the power of Buddhism, the power of faith, the power of passion you display.

You are never defeated. You are never beaten by ridicule or venomous attacks.

Never being defeated is itself victory; it means you have already won. One who lives one's life in such a way is a true victor.

Mothers possess a wisdom and compassion more profound than mere knowledge or theory.

Knowledge is the water pump, while wisdom is the water. Accordingly, those who possess wisdom have a tremendous understanding of human beings and human life.

It is not vast volumes of theory, but profound compassion that makes you a spiritual victor.

Your eyes, turned unwaveringly towards the horizon of kosen-rufu, shine with the unchanging passion of your youth.

Our women's division members, the mothers of kosen-rufu, regard their daily efforts to advance our cause as a sublime and noble duty.

The compassion that resides within a mother's heart is vaster and deeper than all existing knowledge.

During the Second World War and its aftermath, it was women who suffered the most and were forced to endure the greatest privations. Husbands died in action and sons were sent off to the battlefront.

Air raids day in and day out rained down firebombs that wrought horrifying death and destruction. Then, after the war, came a dismal period of dire poverty and near-starvation. Though the war was over, another fierce battle began—as people strove to survive and live with human dignity.

Many were the women who sorrowfully received the remains of beloved husbands or sons killed in action. Their lives and daily experiences were filled with bitter tears. It was an existence of endless hell.

My mentor Josei Toda dedicated his life to the struggle to open the great path leading to security, fulfilment and happiness for women such as these.

"I want to rid the world of misery!"—this ardent desire was the core of President Toda's philosophy.

Should the severe trials of life simply be accepted as destiny? No—our goal as human beings should be to transform our destiny, to eradicate misery from our lives and to accomplish our human revolution so that we can savour lasting joy, happiness and abundant good fortune. Isn't that why you willingly chose to take on this demanding, yet exhilarating, struggle?

Our lives are definitely not limited to this present existence; they are eternal throughout the three existences—past, present and future. As long as we forge an inner state of life of complete happiness and freedom, there is nothing to fear, whatever might happen or wherever we are.

The American Renaissance philosopher Henry David Thoreau once said: "We live a short period of time in this world, but we live it according to the laws of eternal life."[1]

Our women's division members are leading just such lives.

"Why me. . .? Why do I have to have such a wretched destiny?" you might at times be tempted to ask.

Never give in to complaint. Never give up.

Though our individual circumstances may be different, the essential fact remains—we are all human beings. The Daishonin teaches: "It is the heart that is important" ('The Strategy of the Lotus Sutra', WND-1, 1000).

How true his words are. Depending on our resolve, on how we set our hearts and minds, we should be able to triumph in life in any way we want. We should be able to become happy. This is borne out by history.

Many of you may have to suffer others calling you poor. But what does it matter if you are poor? The vast majority of triumphant heroes who left behind magnificent achievements were poor —so poor that they were scorned and ridiculed by others! However, they resolutely took their place on life's stage and won.

Do not become subservient.

Do not dwell on every tiny setback you may encounter in the course of pursuing your chosen path. That would be foolish. Victory or defeat is determined by our entire life. Moreover, our final years are the most crucial.

Those born into a poor family should regard this as their highest honour. They have inherited the baton of fundamental victory as human beings.

What is enviable about the pretentious rich? What is great about conceited celebrities? What is admirable about political leaders who gained their positions of power by treating others with contempt?

Dig where you stand! Remember that there lies a rich wellspring. If you cannot compete in terms of wealth, win in the realm of the heart!

If you cannot compete in terms of social position, win with your profound philosophy!

Happiness is not determined by wealth, good looks or birth.

A world of difference separates outer splendour from spiritual greatness. The crown of the victor shines only in the confident hearts of those who have gained a deep and unshakeable inner awakening to life's truths.

My friends! Do not heed slanderous lies motivated by vile jealousy! You must live with optimism and joy!

There are those who repeatedly trample on others and cast them aside, even though they know they are only hurting themselves infinite times more by doing so—what human folly!

Evil people will return to the hell from whence they came.

Victors shall continue to tread the path of victors.

Again today, our mothers of kosen-rufu strive with selfless dedication. No matter how tired or exhausted they are, they continue to give their all. How commendable and noble they are!

The members of the women's division exert themselves wholeheartedly, with a prayer to eradicate all traces of misery and suffering from the lives of their friends.

How touching is the sincere devotion of these women who intrepidly make their way through life. They brave the fiercest of storms and forge ahead on roads strewn with fallen trees and branches and all manner of obstacles, day after day, year after year, cheerfully singing their own song.

Whether in a famous city or a little known town, or in an exclusive suburb or a poor community, wherever the mothers of kosen-rufu carry out their activities, there the banners of human happiness and victory soar high. There the heroines of our grand drama for peace and justice shine.

Congratulations on this day [10 June] that celebrates the anniversary of the women's division, the foremost gathering of women in the world!

10 June 2004

(*Kosen-rufu Our Mission,* [New Delhi:
Eternal Ganges Press, 2013], vol. 2, 156-62)

Notes:

1. Henry David Thoreau, cited in Leo Tolstoy's A Calendar of Wisdom, translated by Peter Sekirin (New York: Scribner, 1997), 40.

The Peerless Women of Soka—Part 2

Mothers—how I love and admire you! When your meagre budget is exhausted and it's leftovers again for dinner, you laugh it off and remain bright and cheerful, like the dauntless heroine of a play. What a genius you are at making ends meet.

Sincere, stouthearted mothers—queens who possess a down-to-earth majesty!

Even when you lose your beloved husband, you hold back your tears and, for the sake of your children, you stand up bravely with the dignity of a Buddha, a bodhisattva, exerting yourself wholeheartedly and challenging all obstacles.

Dashing away your tears of pain and sorrow, you rise to your feet with firm purpose. How dazzling is your smile! You are a picture of true human victory.

Strong mothers! Gentle mothers! Beautiful mothers! Adored mothers!

With resolute dignity, you keep striving anew for the security and victory of your family and loved ones. You are an indomitable champion of life's drama!

Day after day, forging close ties with your friends and fellow members, you set out with a cheerful sense of purpose to accomplish kosen-rufu, visiting one person after another. You live your life with optimism and joy, your sights set on a glorious future of hope and triumph. How strong you are! You don't know the meaning of the words *defeat* or *surrender*.

Ordinary, yet extraordinary mothers! How sincere and tirelessly hardworking you are. Young mothers! Old mothers!

Mothers, a philosopher once proclaimed, deserve heaven's greatest honours. So do you, our mothers of kosen-rufu.

The dear mothers of our movement who have passed away, too, live on vividly in my heart, a fond, unchanging memory.

Mothers more regal than monarchs. Mothers more noble than aristocrats. Mothers more wise and exemplary than eminent scholars. Mothers more illustrious than any national hero.

You do not hunger for fame or position. Still, it never occurs to the nation's leaders to honour society's nameless mothers, while they heap awards and decorations upon themselves.

How selfless are mothers—seeking nothing for themselves, demanding nothing for themselves.

So vast is your love and compassion that you are ready to give your all, sacrifice all, if need be, as you walk the path of true and genuine devotion with a deep, blazing hope and joy.

A philosopher once said: "Inflicting suffering on mothers is the gravest offence. Those who cause mothers pain are worse than criminals." And a famous novelist once declared: "Despicable are those who bring grief to mothers. They are inhumane beasts, monsters."

The smiles, the happy tears, the rejoicing of mothers—these are the true symbols of happiness, peace and victory.

You, the ordinary, unsung mothers have risen into action. Setting forth from the humble castle that is your home, you have plunged bravely into the tempestuous seas of society to begin your determined struggle. You have begun to charge ahead intrepidly, your life fusing with the dynamic rhythm of the law of the universe —for the sake of peace, for the sake of happiness, for the sake of kosen-rufu.

Mothers! You are the sun of your family—no, you are the sun of the entire world. No matter how dark or dire the circumstances, your presence ensures that bright smiles will never disappear. Where you are, there are no harsh words of pain and anger. Every inch of your home is transformed into a warm and vibrant castle of sparkling hope. How gifted you are at enveloping all in an atmosphere of joy. Your life is free of empty, hypocritical charades of vanity and conceit.

A well-known thinker remarked: "Mothers are great leaders. It is they, not the men of the family, who quietly, briskly and impartially reconcile everyone's disparate wishes and desires."

How beautiful is the smile of a humble, ordinary mother. Not even the world's most famous actress can compare.

How fearsome is a mother's anger. Not even the world's most relentless prosecutor can compare.

Such are the mothers of kosen-rufu, foremost in all the world, burning with a passion of molten steel. Absolutely no one, however great or exalted, can hold a candle to them.

Mothers are a moral compass always pointing true north. Exemplars of upright conduct, they deplore dishonesty and wrongdoing.

A poet once asserted that not treasuring our mothers but causing them pain is a sign of the greatest disrespect. He denounced those who do so, irrespective of their outward splendour, as little better than mindless animals.

Mothers, how wonderful you are. You nurture delicate blossoms of love and hope, conjure happiness and tranquillity as if by magic, and bring unsurpassed joy to your family with your sunny presence.

Like a great stateswoman, you teach the values of justice and duty, while planting in people's hearts the flowers of life's infinite value, the flowers of hope and the flowers of victory.

Mothers of kosen-rufu!

How noble you are, studying the immortal writings of Nichiren Daishonin.

How beautiful you are, praying deeply for the happiness and peace of all humankind.

How majestic you are, striving to advance kosen-rufu, your efforts sparkling with sincerity and courage.

How wondrous you are, giving guidance in faith and Gosho lectures far more inspiring and understandable than any high priest, your words instilling courage and conviction in all.

A certain scholar proclaimed that the priesthood should learn from your fine example.

As election time arrives again in Japan, you dauntlessly defend your political participation, crying: "This is our civic right. We have to use it if we want to change society for the better. No one has any right to criticise our activities." You have an unwavering sense of justice and your position is absolutely correct.

Your evaluation of the candidates is also keen and relentless. You are quick to spot when someone has no drive, or is arrogant, self-centred, unconvincing or over emotional. "I'd like that candidate to work harder at his human revolution," you declare. Your clamorous criticisms ring out day and night.

Your penetrating insights into society and politics are astonishing. And your views on education, peace and many other crucial issues, are far more persuasive than those held by politicians of any stripe. What superb theorists and political scientists you are.

There is no more terrible a dressing-down than one driven by a mother's fury. Her angry rebukes pierce the hearts of her husband and children alike. A judge passing sentence on a defendant cannot hope to stir the same emotions of remorse and repentance as she does with her compassionate scolding, her voice charged with profound anger, sharp yet gentle, strict yet warm. I can see many a husband begging for leniency.

Mothers are experts possessing a wisdom infinitely more solid and profound than the most talented teacher.

There are people who, having thoroughly ridiculed us for our faith, are now happily practising the Daishonin's Buddhism themselves. There are people who, having painted us as villains and spoken ill of us to our neighbours and friends, are now joyfully striving in faith alongside us.

Among even the most vociferous critics who swore they would never join the Soka Gakkai, there are those who today sincerely regret their former words. With the deepest respect for our mothers of kosen-rufu, they are energetically exerting themselves in faith in pursuit of life's highest goal. Hundreds, thousands, hundreds of thousands—indeed, millions—of such people abound today.

Our mothers have won. They have won an exhilarating victory.

Our movement will continue to unfold this way in the future —of that there is no doubt.

One mother—the mother of the Chinese Revolution, Soong Ching-ling—cried: "If the people unite, they can transform everything and move in the direction of peace."[1]

10 June 2004

(Kosen-rufu Our Mission, [New Delhi: Eternal Ganges Press, 2013], vol. 2, 163-67)

Note:

1. Translated from Japanese. Soong Ching-ling, *So Keirei Senshu—Shin Chugoku no tame no Tatakai* (Selected Writings of Soong Ching-ling—The Struggle for the New China), translated by the Institute of Chinese Affairs (Chugoku Kenkyusho) (Tokyo: Hato Shobo, 1953), 312.

The Peerless Women of Soka—Part 3

I recently met a wonderful woman and mother—Madame Laureana San Pedro Rosales, the founder of Capitol University in the Philippines. Madame Rosales is a survivor of the Bataan Death March, an atrocity perpetrated by the Japanese military during their invasion and occupation of the Philippines during the Second World War. Having managed to endure the hellish tragedy and barbarism of the war, Madame Rosales made a resolute vow. Education is the key, she decided, the only way to bring about true peace.

She is a great woman who has devoted her life to fostering people dedicated to peace, an unchanging commitment she has cherished these many decades up to her present age of 79. I met her on June 6, the birthday of first Soka Gakkai president Tsunesaburo Makiguchi.

"The word *surrender* is not in my dictionary" and "Never put off until tomorrow what you can do today"—Madame Rosales has based her life on positive mottos such as these. Mothers are strong, undefeated, undeterred and determined to live out each day to the fullest. Her indomitable will to survive has triumphed and she has surmounted all obstacles.

Madame Rosales visited the Soka International Women's Center in Shinanomachi, Tokyo, accompanied by her daughter,

Dr. Fe Rosales-Juarez, executive vice president and member of the board of trustees of Capitol University, and her son-in-law, Capitol University president and director Casimiro Juarez Jr. As Madame Rosales toured the centre, she said to the women's division members showing her around that she was sure the world would be a better place if the number of Soka women increased— the highest possible accolade for the women's division's network for peace.

In one of his plays, the internationally acclaimed Norwegian dramatist Henrik Ibsen (1828–1906) has the leading male character say: "It is you women that are the pillars of society."[1]Immediately afterwards, a female character responds: "The spirit of truth and the spirit of freedom—they are the pillars of society."[2]

The times are beginning to grow more disordered and chaotic as dark jealousy and envy run rampant. A decent, honest life is threatened on all sides by countless perils. People twist the truth. They resent and envy anyone who demonstrates character and integrity. They have lost all sense of right and wrong.

Shakespeare warned: "Time shall unfold what plighted cunning hides; / Who cover faults, at last shame them derides."[3]

Now, in accord with Nichiren Daishonin's assertion that "When great evil occurs, great good follows" ('Great Evil and Great Good', WND-1, 1119), the time has come for humanity to shine once again. The only way that we can usher in such an age is by pressing forward with unshakeable confidence and unflagging hope in our efforts to transform society where hostile and vindictive human relations abound. In other words, good, strong people need to stand up as new pillars of hope and courage for society.

Those who win in the end are the true and lasting victors.

The Daishonin notes: "Shakyamuni Buddha said that a person who observes filial piety deserves to be called a World-Honored One" ('King Rinda', WND-1, 990). People who care deeply for their mothers and strive to repay their gratitude to them are true World-Honoured Ones and Buddhas.

When mothers came to him seeking the Buddhist teaching, Shakyamuni welcomed them with the utmost respect and warmth. He felt immense compassion and concern for women and mothers. That is precisely why his enemies, who were jealous of his lofty character, tried to use women in the foul and malicious plots they devised to entrap him.

Two of the nine great ordeals experienced by the Buddha were slanders involving women—the slander of Sundari and the slander of Chincha. In both cases, a group of Brahmans, envious of the morally irreproachable Shakyamuni and afraid that they would lose the offerings they lived on, persuaded a corrupt woman to make false charges against him. They then widely publicised these malicious lies, presenting them as fact. Naturally, in the end, the truth was revealed and Shakyamuni's innocence was demonstrated beyond a shadow of a doubt. The villains who had slandered him were severely punished and, of course, brought about their own ruin, suffering in the hellish fires of karma.

In contrast, one female practitioner who had gone through many vicissitudes alongside the Buddha declared proudly that Shakyamuni had triumphed over all, dispelled the devilish influences and was indomitable. She proclaimed that this worthy person was her teacher and that she gladly dedicated herself to the Dharma that he preached.

In a letter to the lay nun Sennichi, the Daishonin writes: "Because they look upon Nichiren, who is trying to save them, as a deadly enemy, these women [women throughout Japan influenced by erroneous priests] all join together to slander him to the ruler of the country, so that, after having been exiled to the province of Izu, he was also exiled to the province of Sado" ('The Sutra of True Requital', WND-1, 932). The Daishonin wished more deeply than anyone for the happiness of women. It is quite likely that if he hadn't struggled so hard to lead them to enlightenment, he may not have been branded with the slanderous charge of being an immoral priest, or repressed by the authorities.

Nevertheless, the Daishonin staunchly endured the momentous persecutions that befell him and selflessly dedicated his life to propagating the Lotus Sutra that "opened up the way to attaining Buddhahood for all women of later ages" ('The Opening of the Eyes-II', WND-1, 269), and the Mystic Law that represented "the sutra of true requital for repaying the kindness of our mother" ('The Sutra of True Requital', WND-1, 931). He thus revealed the path by which all people could repay their gratitude to their mothers into the eternal future.

The Daishonin's female followers in turn prayed earnestly for his safety and well-being, wishing to ensure his protection even if it should cost them their own lives. The Daishonin went so far as to praise these sincere followers as having even stronger resolve than his own. In addition, he bestowed the title of "Sage" on a woman who came to visit him on the island of Sado, bringing her child with her, and affixed the title of "Venerable" to the name of a woman who continued to strive valiantly in her faith even after losing her beloved son. The Daishonin lauded his women disciples who persevered amid great adversity: "The moon of your mind is without shadow and all stain has vanished from your body. You are a Buddha in your present body— how wonderful, how wonderful!" ('Reply to the Lay Nun Kōnichi', WND-2, 1068)

The Decline of the Law Sutra predicts a time when evil priests will corrupt the Buddhist teachings and sow confusion. The Daishonin frequently quoted from this sutra as textual proof of the defiled age of the Latter Day of the Law. A passage from the sutra states: "When the Law is on the verge of decline, women will be diligent in their practice and attain benefit, while men will be lazy and arrogant and not pay heed to the Law." In other words, when the correct teaching of Buddhism is on the brink of being lost, women will come forward and practise with great fervour, do good deeds and create abundant benefit. Men, on the other hand, will be lazy and arrogant and ignore the true teachings.

In an evil age filled with villainous people seeking to destroy Buddhism, women's sharp sense of justice, their moral integrity, their sincerity and their other wonderful qualities will shine. Women are playing the leading role in protecting the correct teaching and doctrines of Buddhism. You, the women of the SGI, are majestic queens of life, experts in the highest wisdom, who are working tirelessly for the welfare and security of all humankind! The strength and power of women is immense; it is unlimited.

In our great journey of kosen-rufu, storms of persecution have beset us repeatedly. Three generations of mentors and disciples have been singled out as the targets of slanders that distorted the truth and sullied justice. At those times, who was it that chanted strong, determined daimoku in an invincible lion's roar for truth? Who was it that courageously and clearly spoke out against falsehood and struck fear into the hearts of the three powerful enemies? It was you, the noble women of SGI.

The integrity, dignity and truth of the mentors and disciples of Soka, heirs to the Buddha's will and decree, have been steadfastly proven and protected by the women's division!

The Daishonin writes: "Worthies and sages are tested by abuse" ('Letter from Sado', WND-1, 303). Numerous baseless rumours were also spread about Chinese premier Zhou Enlai, a dedicated leader of the people and a man of spotless character. Some claimed, for instance, that he had illegitimate children hidden away here and there. Madame Deng Yingchao, Premier Zhou's wife and companion in struggle, has attested to the purity of his character and actions.

I am reminded of some words of encouragement she gave to one of her comrades: "The lotus emerges unstained from the mud to bloom with a refined and noble elegance."[4] She further said: "When we were faced with adversity [back in the days of the revolution], didn't we fight with all our might . . . ? Leaving our homes, we never knew if we'd return again safely. . . . In times of hardship, we must keep looking ahead, we must find hope, we must find light."⁵ These words resonate perfectly with the struggle of the SGI women's division. The lives of our pioneering women members in particular are brilliant examples of the principle of "lotus flowers blooming in the muddy water".

SGI has now spread to 188 countries and territories [currently 192], and the women's division has become the strongest and most admirable women's organisation in the world, advancing at the forefront of peace and culture. The leaders of the SGI in every country all agree on the strength and dynamism of the women's division. Kosen-rufu is indeed advancing through the power of women.

On 5 May, I welcomed a group of 12 women's division members from SGI-Bolivia. Beautiful tears of emotion sparkled on their noble faces, which revealed their triumph over hardship. Their fathers and mothers rode tens of kms on bicycles and horses through the harsh environment of their country to spread the Daishonin's Buddhism; sometimes when they tried to convey their message to fellow frontier farmers in the Bolivian jungle, they were driven away with machetes! These women, carrying on their parents' mission from the time of their youth, have advanced along the same difficult and demanding path of pioneers.

Kosen-rufu cannot be accomplished by lamenting over the difficult circumstances we face; we must win where we are now, in our daily lives! When we change, our environment also changes dramatically. That is the principle of human revolution.

"I will not be defeated! I will be victorious!"—when we make this resolve our guiding spirit, every difficulty we encounter will become a springboard for our human revolution, a treasure adorning our lives.

SGI-Bolivia has achieved tremendous development. Its membership has increased 20-fold since the establishment of its first chapter [in 1962]. The young women's division and young men's division, the successors of the next generation, have also grown splendidly. In addition, SGI-Bolivia's activities for peace and culture are earning growing support and understanding from Bolivian society.

"Tenacity is the mark of greatness."[6] These words of the renowned Bolivian writer Franz Tamayo (1879–1956) are indeed an appropriate tribute to the women's division.

Nichiren Daishonin writes: "Our mother [may be likened to] the earth" ('The Sutra of True Requital', WND-1, 930). The strength of mothers is the strength of the earth. Just as the earth embraces the mountains and enfolds the rivers, the accepting embrace of mothers is infinite and all-encompassing. Just as the earth enables plants to flourish, flowers to bloom and fruit to grow, so mothers are the all-nurturing earth of creativity and education. When mothers move into action, everything changes. Mothers can transform their families, their communities, their society and the age in which they live. It is also mothers who will transform our world into a realm of peace.

A great mother of the Philippines, Madame Rosales, has said that if you apply yourself with sincerity and devotion, you will succeed at whatever you do. This is absolutely true. The sincere efforts of the women of Soka are certain to result in victory! Without the slightest doubt, they will lead to triumph!

15 June 2004
(Kosen-rufu Our Mission, [New Delhi:
Eternal Ganges Press, 2013], vol. 2, 168-74)

Notes:

1. Henrik Ibsen, *The Pretenders, Pillars of Society, Rosmersholm,* translated by R. Farquharson Sharp (London: J. M. Dent & Sons, Ltd., 1955), 227.

2. Ibid.

3. William Shakespeare, *King Lear,* in *William Shakespeare: The Complete Works* (New York: Gramercy Books, 1975), Act I, Scene 1, 976.

4. Translated from Chinese. Jin Feng, *Deng Yingchao zhuan* (Biography of Deng Yingchao) (Beijing: Renmin chubanshe, 1993), 635.

5. Ibid.

6. Translated from Spanish. Franz Tamayo, *Obra escogida,* edited by Mariano Baptista Gumucio (Caracas: Biblioteca Ayacucho, 1979), 138.

Like Flowers of the Field

O ne morning, I heard my wife softly singing to herself—a song at once familiar and at the same time completely fresh to my ears:

> Like flowers of the field,
> tossed by the wind.
> Like flowers of the field,
> delighting all who see.

"What's that song?" I asked.

"It's quite famous," she replied. It was 'Flowers of the Field',[1] a beautiful melody that had been made popular by the Japanese husband-and-wife duo Da Capo.

Smiling, my wife continued:

> Like flowers of the field,
> beaten by the rain.
> Like flowers of the field,
> soothing all who see.

"What a nice song," I said. "It captures the heroic spirit of ordinary people." Hearing it set me quietly contemplating.

'Flowers of the field'—the name of no specific flower is mentioned in the lyrics. This might be a good thing. Different people living in different places have different images of "flowers of the field". For instance, in Japan, we might picture cudweed or cymbidium orchids, or violets or field mustard blossoms or lilies, or cosmos.

The north country is still under a deep blanket of snow. When the snow finally melts and the first shoots of Japanese butterbur and amur adonis begin to appear at the foot of the mountains, people's hearts will leap with joy, knowing that spring has come.

The Echizen daffodil grows even on the steep cliffs facing the pounding waves of the Japan Sea, enduring winter's fierce winds until spring arrives.

Hiroshima and Nagasaki were devastated by the atom bomb. People thought it would be decades before plant life could grow once more in its scorched earth. But oleanders quickly bloomed there again, bringing hope and courage to the survivors struggling to rebuild their lives.

I think we all have an image in our hearts of hardy flowers of the field blooming cheerfully, undaunted by wind or rain.

Whether noticed or not, these wildflowers, in the place where they have taken root, put forth stems, spread their leaves and flower beautifully, each in their own distinct way. Some bloom by the wayside in such inconspicuous and incongruous places that they invite our astonishment and admiration for their strength and tenacity. I have frequently photographed such blossoms, pressing the shutter as a way of applauding their unheralded efforts.

"'Flowers of the Field'—why, it's the perfect anthem for our women's division," I commented.

Nodding in agreement, my wife said: "Yes. As a matter of fact, it was a women's division member from Meguro who told me about the song in a letter she sent me."

The woman, it turned out, was a member of the first graduating class of Kansai Soka Junior and Senior High Schools. She had been struggling hard, doing her best to care for a daughter afflicted with a chronic illness. She had been chanting earnestly and forging ahead valiantly, one day after another without rest or respite. Then she heard this song and began to sing it to herself:

> Life is sometimes filled with hardships,
> But rainy and cloudy days, too, are followed by sunshine,
> That's when you appreciate
> the dauntless spirit of flowers of the field.

"Dauntless spirit"—surely that is another way of describing courage. Life is a series of on-going challenges; it is a struggle to bring the flowers of happiness into bloom, regardless of the difficulties we may face along the way.

My wife, her eyes bright with emotion and her words full of praise and admiration, is always recounting to me the courageous struggles and noble victories of our women's and young women's division members in different parts of Japan and throughout the world.

Once during a visit to Hyogo Prefecture in the Kansai region, I shared a poem I had read in my childhood:

Trampled
and trampled again
still it blooms—
the smiling dandelion.[2]

This poem is a wonderful description of the many ordinary men and women who bravely live out their lives, a smile on their faces, no matter what hardship and adversity they encounter.

Why isn't the dandelion defeated by constant trampling? The key to its strength is its long and sturdy root, which extends deep into the earth. Dandelions may have a taproot more than one full metre in length.

The same principle applies to people. The true victors in life are those who, enduring repeated challenges and setbacks, have sent the roots of their being to such a depth that nothing can shake them. The German writer Schiller captured this image perfectly in *The Maid of Orleans,* his play about Joan of Arc, in the phrase: "O beauteous flower of victory!"[3]

On 12 February, the 3,000th instalment of *The New Human Revolution* was published. The heroines of this novel are ordinary women. Some of the characters are based on women living in foreign countries, wracked by homesickness, weeping as they gazed over the seas towards their land of birth. Encountering the Mystic Law, these women rose to the challenge of transforming their own karma and courageously embarked on a new life as proud pioneers of worldwide kosen-rufu. Around the globe and in Japan, these intrepid Soka women struggled bravely against illness, accidents, economic hardship, family discord and a host of other problems. Overcoming one painful, trying obstacle after another, they created great dramas of personal victory exemplifying Nichiren Daishonin's words: "[W]inter always turns to spring" ('Winter Always Turns into Spring', WND-1, 536). Today, these women are enjoying truly wonderful golden years, overflowing with happiness and good fortune.

In contrast, arrogant individuals or groups who ridiculed and inflicted pain on these noble women of kosen-rufu have, as we all know, sunk into utter obscurity. As the Daishonin declared: "In the past, and in the present Latter Day of the Law, the rulers, high ministers and people who despise the votaries of the Lotus Sutra seem to be free from punishment at first, but eventually they are all doomed to fall" ('On Persecutions Befalling the Sage', WND-1, 997). These are stern and uncompromising words.

Our pioneering Soka women have been uncrowned ordinary citizens, without special social status, wealth or fame. And it is these very women who have built the Soka Gakkai into the great organisation it is today. Buddhism exists so that these women can become happy.

The Daishonin declares that in the Lotus Sutra "the enlightenment of women is expounded as a model [for the enlightenment of all living beings]" ('The Sutra of True Requital', WND-1, 930). Buddhism teaches that women who have made the greatest efforts, who are challenging themselves the most, will be wreathed in unsurpassed flowers of happiness. This is the brilliant path to happiness for all women struggling with hardship and difficulties in the real world.

A poet wrote:

> Gaze down calmly
> on washed-out pretenders,
> and follow your own
> flower-adorned path
> without regret.

Wildflowers are neither vain nor haughty, neither jealous nor servile. Living in accord with their unique mission, characterising the Buddhist principle of 'cherry, peach, plum and damson blossoms', they neither envy other flowers nor belittle themselves. They take pride in their identity, knowing that each is a flower with a bloom like no other.

Even the prettiest and most delicate wildflowers are by no means weak. They may seem fragile, but they are strong. They are not perturbed by rain or wind. Embodying the same indomitable spirit, our motto is "Nothing can defeat us!"

My wife, too, regards the frontline struggles for kosen-rufu she has carried out since her youth as her greatest pride and honour. When the youth division was established in July 1951 by President

Toda, I was a young men's division group chief and my wife was a young women's division group chief. The following month, a new young woman joined the Soka Gakkai, and my wife visited her home to enshrine her Gohonzon. My wife was younger than her, but senior in faith. She became close to the young woman and did her utmost to be there for her, listening to her problems, offering advice and encouraging her. That member grew tremendously and became a young women's division leader herself. Later, she went on to serve admirably as one of the top leaders of the women's division until the end of her life.

During the historic February Campaign of 1952, the youth division, burning with the spirit of refuting the erroneous and revealing the true, held a study presentation meeting with President Toda attending. My wife rose to the podium as a representative of the young women's division and gave a presentation on the erroneous belief that personal misfortune was caused by the negative workings of deceased spirits, an idea that was especially popular among several of the new religions that appeared in Japan after the Second World War. She explained the issues with great clarity and resoundingly debunked the idea.

A smiling Mr. Toda watched warmly over my wife and the other young women. It was his conviction that the growing strength of the young women's division members based on Buddhist study is the flower of hope of kosen-rufu.

Renowned Kenyan environmental activist Wangari Maathai took time out of her extremely busy schedule during her recent trip to Japan to visit me at the Seikyo Shimbun building on 18 February. The founder of the Green Belt Movement, Dr. Maathai is a "green crusader" who was awarded the Nobel Peace Prize last year (2004).

Members of the Soka University Pan-African Friendship Society welcomed Dr. Maathai with a rendition of the Kenyan song 'This Is Our Home'.[4] Dr. Maathai sang along cheerfully as she swayed to the music's infectious rhythm:

> This is our home.
> Our aim is to plant trees here.
> Our home is a home of womenfolk.
> Come, let's carry the tree seedlings and plant.

In the past, the Green Belt Movement was persecuted, and Dr. Maathai herself was jailed for her activism on several occasions. She was even tortured. Throughout everything, and while raising three children, she courageously acted on her beliefs in her effort to break the vicious cycle of poverty and environmental destruction.

I have heard that the first seven trees Dr. Maathai ever planted were African tulip trees, known for their fiery red flowers. The red flame of courage burning in her heart has, over the last three decades, kindled similar flames in the hearts of over 100,000 people, while the planting of those first seven trees has led to more than 30 million trees being planted.

In *A Quiet Revolution,* a film on environmental issues produced with the cooperation of the SGI, Dr. Maathai says: "It is very important for us to take action at the local level, because sometimes when we think of the global problems, we get disempowered, but when we take action at the local level, we are empowered."

These words resonate with the philosophy that drives the grass-roots activities and networks of our women's and young women's divisions. That is why Dr. Maathai has also expressed her sincere empathy with our Soka philosophy and movement, which values the individual and society, and life and the environment.

Dr. Maathai, who herself espouses a philosophy of hope, has declared: "We know that the little we are doing is making positive change. If we can multiply that several million times, we can change the world—definitely." It is just as she says.

We need to continue expanding our network of "flowers of the field", bringing one blossom after another into harmonious and happy bloom. This is how we will achieve a truly spectacular "quiet revolution" in the century of women. Harmony is life's greatest beauty, its flower.

I remember an incident that took place many years ago, when the Soka Gakkai was still a small organisation. My mentor Josei Toda's business was in dire straits: we had no money, no capable staff and were at rock bottom. One day, Mr. Toda suddenly plucked a flower nearby and put it in my shirt pocket, as if it were a medal of honour. I was spending my days striving desperately and completely alone to serve, fight for and protect my mentor. Mr. Toda said to me: "I'm sorry for all the trouble I've caused you. You're really doing a fine job, Daisaku." Some snickered at my floral medal of honour, but to me it was an award for kosen-rufu presented by my mentor in kosen-rufu. No tribute could have been greater.

When I returned to my shabby apartment, I placed the flower before the Gohonzon and chanted daimoku with deep gratitude. I still wear my mentor's floral medal of honour in my heart, and I continue my struggle in the same spirit as that youth so long ago. The flower my mentor bestowed on me has now been transformed into 23 shining national medals of honour from countries around the world.

Buddhism says that the disciple is like the plant and the teacher, the earth.[5] It also sets forth the path of repaying debts of gratitude, explaining that the flowers of victory brought to bloom by the disciple will return to the earth as good fortune for the mentor, and that new flowers of victory will be born from the earth of mentor and disciple.[6] My wife and I are proud to have followed this path throughout our lives. Our foremost wish is to bestow all our sincere, dedicated Soka women with a floral crown of happiness that sparkles brighter than any jewel-encrusted tiara. We wish to present them with a floral crown of absolute victory, a floral crown of eternity, happiness, true self and purity.

Our conversation that morning began with a song about flowers of the field.

"Another day of fresh challenges lies ahead of us, doesn't it?" my wife said.

"That's right!" I responded. "Let's keep working for the happiness and victory of ordinary people, who are the most precious of all!"

A smile blossomed on my wife's face like a lovely flower.

The flowers of the field, too,
rise up excitedly:
"Spring is here! Spring!"

5 March 2005

(*Kosen-rufu Our Mission*, New Delhi:
Eternal Ganges Press 2013, vol. 2, 175-83)

Notes:

1. Japanese title "No ni Saku Hana no yo ni". Lyrics by Masami Sugiyama and music by Ase Kobayashi. Released in 1983, it was the theme song of a popular Japanese television series.

2. A well-known Japanese verse; author anonymous.

3. Friedrich von Schiller, 'The Maid of Orleans', in Schiller's *Complete Works*, translated by Charles J Hempel (Philadelphia: I Kohler, 1861), (vol. 1, 'The Entity of the Mystic Law', 418).

4. "Guku ni Gwitu".

5. Referring to his teacher Dozen-bo, the Daishonin writes: "Nichiren is like the plant, and my teacher, the earth" ('Flowering and Bearing Grain', WND-1, 909).

6. In the same writing, he states: "The rice plant flowers and bears grain, but its spirit remains in the soil. This is the reason the stalk sprouts to flower and bear grain once again. The blessings that Nichiren obtains from propagating the Lotus Sutra will always return to Dozen-bo. How sublime!" (WND-1, 909). Elsewhere, he also says: "Thus the flower will return to the root, and the essence of the plant will remain in the earth. The benefit that I have been speaking of will surely accumulate in the life of the late Dozen-bo" ('On Repaying Debts of Gratitude', WND-1, 737).

Saluting the Women's Division—Part 1

A life
lived with
limitless hope
is the path of happiness,
the path of Soka.

In this month of June, celebrating the anniversary of its founding, our incomparable women's division is making great strides forward with brilliant vigour and optimism.

The French author Victor Hugo (1802–85) wrote in his masterpiece *Les Misérables:* "What is the sun? It is love. Who says love says woman. Aha! There is an omnipotence; it is woman."[1] There is also a magnificent sun in the Soka Gakkai—the women's division. Our unrivalled women's division is an incredible force for peace.

June 10 is Women's Division Day. On this day in 1951, just after my mentor Josei Toda had been inaugurated as the second president of the Soka Gakkai (on May 3), the organisation's leading women's representatives assembled with him to make a fresh start with the founding of a new division. When I think of the fact that this division was established a month before the young men's and young women' divisions, I see what immense respect Mr. Toda had for our women members.

When the mothers of Soka are as firm and sound as the earth, youth can grow vigorously into mighty trees. When the mothers of Soka shine with hope, youth can advance in high spirits. This is an unchanging truth.

The light of the sun, known by ancients as the "eye of the heavens", brightly illuminates the earth and dispels the darkness. Mothers, too, seem to possess a penetrating light, an all-seeing power, as far as their families are concerned! Women often tend to be keen judges of character. They can see through people, quickly spotting phonies behind the screen of fancy words and phrases. They are always focussed on the true nature of things. Nothing escapes their perceptive gaze.

Many women's division members are extremely busy. On top of household responsibilities, they devote their energies not only to raising and caring for their children but also to fostering the members of the future division. In addition, many have jobs and careers outside the home and are actively involved in their local communities. There are also those who, though suffering from personal bereavement, continue to do their best to help others. The women's division members exert themselves tirelessly for the happiness and welfare of their friends and fellow members. They are truly carrying out the work of Buddhas and bodhisattvas.

Even if no one is aware of your exertions for kosen-rufu, the heavenly deities—the positive forces of the universe—will surely protect you. The Buddhist teaching that, though unseen by others, our efforts are definitely observed by all Buddhas and bodhisattvas, is absolutely true. As a result, unimaginably great benefit is certain to bloom forth and brilliantly adorn the lives of our dedicated women's division members.

The beautiful and joyous network of the women's division, which started in Japan 58 years ago with only 52 members, has now spread around the world. We live in an unprecedented age where there are SGI women's division members all throughout the globe who champion our lofty cause and vigorously chant daimoku for world peace and the happiness of themselves and others.

One of the pioneers of worldwide kosen-rufu whom I will never forget is Rosa Kishimoto, former women's division leader and women's division senior executive leader of SGI-Peru. She has dedicated her all to kosen-rufu. While living very modestly, she has exerted herself earnestly day in and day out to offer encouragement to members. I have a lasting impression of her refined inner radiance and quiet dignity, qualities of a life polished by faith. She is a role model for other women leaders.

Witnessing Mrs. Kishimoto's sincerity and commitment during my second visit to Peru 35 years ago (in 1974), I was inspired to share her story later with a Japanese women's magazine.

Mrs. Kishimoto is the Peruvian-born daughter of Japanese immigrants. She is open and accepting of everyone. Basing herself on the egalitarian teaching of Nichiren Daishonin's Buddhism, she has reached out to others naturally and without prejudice, forging close friendships with a large number of people. Because of strained circumstances inflicted on her family by the outbreak of the Second World War, she was only able to complete elementary school. But she has always bravely and unhesitatingly engaged in dialogue with others, no matter who they are. With her fundamental belief in human equality, she has made friends with people of different backgrounds and walks of life. Even now, this ordinary woman who is loved as the "mother of kosen-rufu in Peru" maintains wide-ranging friendships with many individuals.

A big challenge facing society today is how to form networks and alliances among people, on both the local and global levels. There has never been a more pressing need than now for people to cooperate in various areas, ranging from resource recycling to caring for children and the elderly. One of the aims of our kosen-rufu movement, too, is to unite people's hearts and build new grassroot networks.

The French thinker Marquis de Vauvenargues (1715–47) wrote: "Becoming familiar with others is training for the spirit."[2] It is through our interactions with others that we develop and forge our character. Human relationships begin with the courage to initiate a dialogue. For some, it means making a conscious effort to break out of their shell, to overcome their tendency to hide away and avoid others' company. Making efforts to talk to and converse with others is the first step in transforming oneself from a closed to an open individual.

Moreover, as Soka Gakkai members, our endeavours to reach out to others and share our philosophy with them are inspired not only by our wish for their happiness but the desire to work together with them in actualising peace and prosperity in our communities and society as a whole. That's why it is so important for us to be people who are not only trustworthy and dependable, but also a source of inspiration to others. We can only do this if we don't succumb to egoism or self-absorption, but keep striving to elevate our state of life day after day.

Please know that this process leads directly to our personal growth and human revolution.

Friendship is a lifetime treasure. To develop beautiful friendships throughout one's life and polish one's life as a result—there is surely no more wonderful existence than this!

This means that our women's division members, masters of the art of friendship, are also experts in bringing forth life's supreme brilliance.

My friends in the women's division, please make full use of that sublime talent and, with bright smiles and through courageous and heartfelt dialogues, build solid alliances in your local areas—alliances of thinking people, alliances of happiness and victory.

My third visit to Peru took place 25 years ago, in 1984. I was overjoyed to be reunited with my fellow members there, dedicated Bodhisattvas of the Earth shining as beacons of hope in their country. On that occasion, Peruvian President Fernando Belaúnde Terry (1912–2002) presented me with the nation's Order of the Sun of Peru in the Grade of Grand Cross. Four days after that ceremony, on the last day of my stay, my wife and I were invited to a luncheon at the president's residence with the president, the first lady, the prime minister, the minister of education and a number of other cabinet members in attendance.

The person who interpreted for me that day was Mrs. Kishimoto. Though she was asked to take on this task at short notice, wanting to support me any way she could, she readily accepted. She had no professional training as an interpreter, much less any experience interpreting for government leaders. It was only natural that she was nervous. But she rose to the occasion with the typical aplomb one has come to associate with women's division members. Perhaps also reassured by my words of encouragement, "You don't need to worry," once the luncheon began she confidently discharged her responsibilities as interpreter, speaking in a calm and dignified voice. When the luncheon finished and I thanked her for the good job she did, she was all smiles.

Once they set their minds to something, women are strong. Nothing can beat the wisdom and quick thinking of women at a crucial moment.

In addition, a hope-filled drama unfolds in a life firmly dedicated to the path of mentor and disciple.

Mrs. Kishimoto regards Peru as her very life. Her devotion to kosen-rufu is an expression of her complete and lifelong commitment to her beloved homeland and the members there. Her spirit resonates with the Daishonin's words: "Life is limited; we must not begrudge it. What we should ultimately aspire to is the Buddha land" ('Aspiration for the Buddha Land', WND-1, 214). Because this invincible determination lies deep within her, Mrs. Kishimoto has been able to encourage her fellow members with a warm smile and dedicate herself to the realisation of kosen-rufu in Peru, unswayed by any obstacle.

Do not lament,
live joyfully!
Mothers of kosen-rufu,
uphold a lofty philosophy
and enjoy life's journey!

Our SGI organisation in Brazil has also won great trust in society. Brazilian President Luiz Inácio Lula da Silva expressed his high hopes for our movement, saying that the people of Brazil are watching and praying for the success of SGI's global activities for peace, culture, education and human rights.[3]

The late Silvia Saito, who served as SGI-Brazil (BSGI) women's division leader and women's division senior executive leader, was a pioneering member who contributed greatly to laying the foundations of the BSGI organisation.

For a long period, Brazil was ruled by a military dictatorship, and because of its misunderstanding of our organisation caused by ungrounded rumours, I was once denied a visa and had to cancel my plans to visit that country (in 1974). During that time, Mrs. Saito made a determination to ensure that I would be able to visit Brazil in the future and vowed to create an age when the entire nation would praise and trust the SGI.

An earnest resolve always leads to earnest action. Mrs. Saito started with powerful prayer. She stirred up a groundswell of daimoku. Many women decided to join her and began chanting purposefully towards the same goal. They also spoke with people in society about the noble ideals of the SGI, the teachings of Buddhism, and the pride of a life committed to the path of mentor and disciple. Most of these women were dealing with their own problems and difficulties—poverty, sickness, trouble with their children and so on. But this did not deter them from their prayers and actions to promote kosen-rufu in Brazil in a spirit of oneness with their mentor.

Nichiren Daishonin writes: "There should be no discrimination among those who propagate the five characters of Myoho-renge-kyo in the Latter Day of the Law, be they men or women. Were they not Bodhisattvas of the Earth, they could not chant the daimoku"

('The True Aspect of Phenomena', WND-1, 385). We are able to dedicate ourselves to kosen-rufu and chant Nam-myoho-renge-kyo because we are Bodhisattvas of the Earth. When we struggle and chant for kosen-rufu, the great life-state of these altruistic bodhisattvas—a life-state of complete fulfilment brimming with joy, hope and courage —pulses within us. This is how we transform our inner state of life. The pure, strong life-force that wells forth as a result enables us to weather and triumph over our personal problems and worries.

As one of the five guidelines of the women's division states, "Everything starts with prayer". It is important to wholeheartedly pray and strive to the very end, taking activities for kosen-rufu as an opportunity to challenge one's problems and change one's karma.

Overcoming our personal problems and achieving personal happiness can be likened to the earth rotating on its axis, while advancing kosen-rufu and thereby contributing to the prosperity of society can be likened to the earth revolving around the sun. Just as these two movements of the earth are inseparable, individual happiness and social prosperity can be achieved in tandem based on the principles of the Daishonin's Buddhism.

The Daishonin declares: "If only you chant Nam-myoho-renge-kyo, then what offense could fail to be eradicated? What blessing could fail to come?" ('Conversation between a Sage and an Unenlightened Man', WND-1, 130). I wish to reaffirm here that we carry out our Gakkai activities not only for the sake of the Law and society, but for our own indestructible happiness as well.

In any event, the praise our movement is winning in Brazilian society is in large part due to the steadfast prayers and actions of the BSGI women's division members.

In 1979, 30 years ago this year, after I was forced to resign as the third president of the Soka Gakkai, the three powerful enemies[4] of Buddhism struck with even greater intensity, seeking to destroy the organisation, which was now without its leader.

It was precisely at that time that the members of Kansai responded to my lion's roar for justice, boldly proclaiming their vow to fight alongside me. They did so with their rousing song at the First Kansai Choral Festival, held at the Soka Gakkai's Kansai Toda Memorial Auditorium in Osaka on 15 July, in the month of mentor and disciple.

In those dark, dark days following my resignation, pressure from the Nichiren Shoshu priesthood and treacherous individuals within our organisation restricted what I could do; I was not allowed to move about freely or offer guidance at meetings and had to virtually disappear from the spotlight. But my precious comrades in Kansai resolved to challenge this adversity. "President Ikeda is with us in our Gakkai songs," they declared. The Gakkai spirit is the shakubuku spirit. And since the pioneering days of our organisation, the spirit of mentor and disciple has been alive in our songs filled with the commitment to widely propagate the Daishonin's Buddhism.

The previous year (1978), I had composed lyrics for 30 new Gakkai songs—songs for various divisions and regions, including the student division's "Kofu ni Hashire"(Onward to Kosen-rufu), the young women's "Seishun Zakura" (Cherry Blossoms of Youth), and Kansai's 'Josho no Sora' (Ever-victorious Skies). The members were not going to let anyone tell them that they couldn't sing these Gakkai songs, which I had written under the pen name Shin'ichi Yamamoto.

On the day of the First Kansai Choral Festival, the members of Kansai, joining me in my struggle, renewed their vow, their powerful voices ringing out again and again. They sang 49 songs at this event, including "Ifu Dodo no Uta" (Song of Indomitable Dignity), which I had composed in Kansai, and the song 'Ha Ha Yo' (Mother), with its beautiful melody, performed by the Kansai women's division. The festival opened and closed with 'Ever-victorious Skies', which had debuted exactly one year earlier. Driving away every dark cloud with their voices, the members sang the lyrics from that song:

> Now again forming our ranks,
> you and I,
> together from the distant past,
> comrades embracing a shared vow,
> sing a song of spring.
> Beloved Kansai, rise courageously!

Among those listening to the joyous voices of these Kansai members was my wife who, sharing my spirit and commitment, represented me at this event.

After the festival, my wife spent several days talking together with Kansai women's division members, including those who had fought alongside me in the Osaka Campaign[5] (in 1956). She also visited women at their homes to offer encouragement. "We will not be defeated," they told her with vividly sparkling eyes. They were filled with a pledge of gratitude.

Having heard a detailed report of these events from my wife, I was confident that Kansai was solid and that the Kansai women's division was in high spirits. The bonds of mentor and disciple still flourished there, so I knew Kansai was secure. In my heart, I called on them: Members of Kansai, comrades from the beginningless past, now is the time to rise up to the challenge and launch a powerful counterattack from Kansai to spur Tokyo to action.

Three decades have passed since then. The flames of the Gakkai spirit that blazed in Kansai spread to Tokyo, the rest of Japan and throughout the world. The Soka mentor-disciple spirit has vanquished all storms of obstacles and devilish forces.

The Ever-victorious Kansai spirit is the eternal treasure of the Soka Gakkai. It is the invincible spirit that refuses to be defeated, always winning against the odds. It is the formidable force of the people that can break through walls of obstacles with the wisdom born of faith. It is the dynamic transformative power that can change any kind of suffering into joy. And as long as the noble ever-victorious women's division members of Kansai are steadfast, the Soka citadel of the people will be unassailable.

When the Ikegami brothers were fighting against persecution, the Daishonin encouraged their wives—predecessors of our women's division members: "If both of you unite in encouraging your husbands' faith, you will follow the path of the dragon king's daughter and become a model for women attaining Buddhahood in the evil latter age" ('Letter to the Brothers', WND-1, 502). When women display fortitude in the face of their family's trials or social adversity, taking action based on faith in the Mystic Law, which has the power to 'change poison into medicine', they never have to give in to misfortune.

Make your way with boundless courage! That is how you can dauntlessly open the supreme path of a life of absolute happiness.

The German musician Clara Schumann (1819–96) wrote: "It does happen so often in life that what seemed so harsh, leads to good fortune later on."[6] She also said: "Many things are won [only] through continuous struggle."[7]

12 June 2009

(*Kosen-rufu Our Mission,* [New Delhi: Eternal Ganges Press, 2013], vol. 2, 184-201)

Notes:

1. Victor Hugo, *Les Misérables*, translated by Lee Fahnestock and Norman MacAfee (New York: New American Library, 1987), 1378.

2. Translated from French. '*Luc de Clapiers, Marquis de Vauvenargues, Réflexions et Maximes*' (Reflections and Maxims), in *Oeuvres de Vauvenargues* (The Works of Vauvenargues) (Geneva: Slatkine Reprints, 1970), 384 (Maxim no. 105).

3. Article in *Seikyo Shimbun*, 23 November 2005.

4. Three powerful enemies: Three types of arrogant people who persecute those who propagate the Lotus Sutra in the evil age after Shakyamuni Buddha's death, described in the 20-line verse section of the 'Encouraging Devotion' (13th) chapter of the *Lotus Sutra*. The Great Teacher Miao-lo (711–782) of China summarises them as arrogant lay people, arrogant priests and arrogant false sages.

5. Osaka Campaign: In May 1956, the Kansai members, rallying around a young Daisaku Ikeda, who had been dispatched by second president Josei Toda to support them, introduced 11,111 households to the practice of the Daishonin's Buddhism. In elections held two months later, the Soka Gakkai-backed candidate in Kansai won a seat in the Upper House, an accomplishment that was thought all but impossible at the time.

6. *Johannes Brahms, Johannes Brahms: Life and Letters*, translated by Josef Eisinger and Styra Avins (Oxford: Oxford University Press, 2001), 259.

7. Berthold Litzmann, *Clara Schumann: An Artist's Life*, translated by Grace E. Hadow (London: Macmillan, 1913), vol. 2, 271.

Saluting the Women's Division—Part 2

Resolve
to triumph
in this life,
spending your days wisely
as experts of happiness.

It was in May last year (2008) that Argentine human rights activist and Nobel Peace laureate Adolfo Pérez Esquivel and his wife Amanda Guerreño came to Japan. They found time in their busy schedule to visit Soka University and although, unfortunately, my wife and I were unable to meet with them, they had a friendly exchange with the students and faculty there. On that occasion, Dr. Pérez Esquivel, who is also a renowned artist, brought a gift of six of his drawings for me. They were portraits of women, and of mothers and children. A tribute to mothers who fight for truth and justice and resolutely protect those they love, they were also a gift for all the women of the SGI.

One of these drawings is of a solid woman whose hands seem to be welcoming all the blessings of this earth. I am told that it is a depiction of Pachamama, or Mother Earth, an Incan goddess. Dr. Pérez Esquivel had a great female figure in his own life who was like a Mother Earth—his grandmother, Eugenia. In my dialogue with this Argentine activist, which is currently being prepared for publication in book form, he shares his memories of his beloved grandmother whom he regards as his personal hero.

Dr. Pérez Esquivel, who lost his mother at an early age, was lovingly raised by his grandmother who exerted an enormous influence on his life. In particular, he noted that she had a keen ability to see through people's pretenses, and discern whether they were good-hearted or conceited. When she saw that someone was dishonest, she would warn her grandson to be on guard against them. She would advise him not to trust people who did not look him straight in the face or who beat around the bush before saying something they didn't want to say.[1] Her words were filled with wise insight into human nature.

The eyes are sometimes called the windows to the mind. When someone is lying to you or harbours ill will towards you, you'll find that they often have trouble looking you in the eye. This especially tends to be the case when the person in question is someone you have done a lot for. You have to be on guard against insincere or duplicitous people.

It is also very sad when individuals lead lives that will cause pain and hurt to their mothers. Nichiren Daishonin writes: "Persons who study the teachings of Buddhism must also [observe the ideal of filial piety and] understand and repay their obligations" ('The Opening of the Eyes-I', WND-1, 228). I hope young people will live out their lives with dignity and integrity while cherishing their mothers in their hearts.

Raised by a woman who could be said to symbolise the wisdom of the people, Dr. Pérez Esquivel has boundless expectations for the women of the SGI. He has shared that he is delighted to see the way they are striving as dedicated protagonists to promote awareness of the problems confronting humanity. Without doubt, he said, it is a hopeful sign for the times.[2]

The network of Soka women is truly a brilliant source of inspiration for the present and the future.

I first met Dr. Pérez Esquivel in December 1995 (in Tokyo). He had at that time expressed a desire to continue our dialogue through correspondence or other means. On the day of his return to Argentina, he sent me a message to the following effect: "When someone I trust is being attacked, insulted or persecuted, I will say nothing to that person. But when that person stops being criticised, I express my dissatisfaction to them because it means they have given up their fight."[3] He also shared a wonderful quote from the great novel *Don Quixote* by Spanish writer Miguel de Cervantes (1547–1616): "The dogs are barking. That means we are riding forth."[4] Interestingly enough, this same quote has been cited to me by many of my friends from around the world, including Club of Rome Honorary President Ricardo Díez-Hochleitner, Brazilian pianist and composer Amaral Vieira, and former Chilean Ambassador to Japan Demetrio Infante Figueroa. Hearts that share the same convictions resonate.

The Daishonin writes: "The three obstacles and four devils will invariably appear, and the wise will rejoice while the foolish will retreat" ('The Three Obstacles and Four Devils', WND-1, 637). In the modern age, we who uphold the Mystic Law are the wise who, undaunted by obstacles, are putting this passage into practice.

More than three decades ago, the military dictatorship that ruled Argentina caused the successive disappearances of a great number of its citizens who were suspected of opposing the regime. By some estimates, as many as 30,000 victims were taken away by the military, never to be seen again. Dr. Pérez Esquivel himself endured 14 months in prison fighting for human rights. When he was detained, it was the courage and quick thinking of his wife that saved his life. She resolutely voiced the truth, stating publicly that the authorities had arrested her husband. Her outcry forced the military to reluctantly admit that they had indeed done so, making it impossible for them to simply declare him missing, which was their usual tactic.

Many years ago, I engaged in a series of dialogues via correspondence with the well-known Japanese journalist and author Yasushi Inoue (1907–91). Mr. Inoue emphasised that all human beings, irrespective of who they are, were born of mothers. He continued: "I am sure I am not alone in believing that it is the mothers of the world who are best qualified to speak out against the conditions prevailing in many lands today."[5]

To create a century of life, a century of human rights, and a century of women, women themselves must speak out decisively. Silence means complicity and submission.

Mothers have a special right to have their voices heard. Nothing can compare with the earnest appeals of mothers. Indeed, nothing can silence the noble voices of women, including the voices of the mothers of Soka calling out for truth and justice.

Women's voices can powerfully influence society and transform the world. It was the attainment of women's suffrage, particularly, which gave women a voice in society, marking the start of a new era in human history. The first country to grant women the right to vote on a national level was New Zealand, 116 years ago in 1893. That year, women, with their newly acquired rights, enthusiastically went to cast their votes in the national election.

One of the key campaigners for women's suffrage in New Zealand was Kate Sheppard (1847–1934). In 1888, five years before women's suffrage was achieved, Mrs. Sheppard drew up 10 reasons why women should have the vote. Among the points she listed were: women are less liable than men to be swayed by mere party feeling, and are inclined to attach great value to uprightness and rectitude of life in a candidate; women are endowed with a more constant solicitude for the welfare of the rising generations, thus giving them a more far-reaching concern for something beyond the present moment; and women tend naturally to exercise more habitual caution, and to feel a deeper interest in the constant preservation of peace, law, and order, and especially in the supremacy of right over might.[6] Today, even more than a century later, many are sure to agree with her evaluation.

> Brimming with
> boundless hope,
> the women's division members
> adorn their lives
> with the radiance of the morning sun.

Next year (2010) will mark the 10th anniversary of the completion of the Soka International Women's Center in Shinanomachi, Tokyo.

As many as 650,000 women members from Japan and overseas have visited the centre so far. It has also welcomed a stream of distinguished guests, including a number of first ladies, United Nations officials, and university rectors. It is my wish that everyone treasure this citadel of peace, happiness and philosophy and further enhance the role it can play in contributing to the realisation of a greater, more expansive network of women.

The original Soka Gakkai Women's Center—now the No. 2 Women's Center—opened 31 years ago on 7 June 1978. At thattime, I dubbed it the "White Lily Castle", with the hope that all the women's division members would be lofty and refined like the white lily and always wear smiles of happiness and victory. With those gathered at the opening, I showed a framed calligraphy by first Soka Gakkai president Tsunesaburo Makiguchi, whose birthday fell the day before (June 6). It featured the words, "Mothers of the Gakkai".

The Soka Gakkai is a noble organisation entrusted with the Buddha's intent and decree to carry out kosen-rufu. To be a member of the Soka Gakkai women's division means having a sublime mission and infinite good fortune and benefit.

The women of Soka sincerely pray for everyone's happiness and victory, and speak out with a lion's roar for truth and justice. They have the wisdom for leading long, healthy lives, and the compassion to foster successors. They are beacons of reassurance for their friends, and engage in courageous and joyous dialogues. They unite in the spirit of "many in body, one in mind," and exert themselves in faith based on the oneness of mentor and disciple. They have made the key points of the women's division's five guidelines—prayer, harmony, successors, community, and experiences in faith—their life's treasure. This is why the women's division members, the mothers of kosen-rufu, are shining as the magnificent suns of the world.

You, too,
as a woman of profound mission,
will be a queen of happiness
of kosen-rufu
throughout the three existences.

Sarah Mejía Gonzales, a Bolivian activist and president of the Association of Women's Civic Committees of Santa Cruz Department, has also expressed her appreciation for the activities of the SGI women, saying she is constantly impressed by their positive attitude toward life and their dedicated contributions to their communities. She further conveyed her wish to continue working together with the members of the SGI to build a better society.[7]

As such words indicate, there are now people all over the world who have high aspirations for the dedicated efforts and compassionate dialogues of the women's division members.

Veronica Toynbee (1894–1980), the wife of British historian Arnold J. Toynbee (1889–1975), sent me a letter in her later years in which she declared that she still had much work left to do. My wife and I feel the same way. I'm constantly telling myself: "This is what I will challenge now." "I still have so much to say." "I still have so much to do." To see every day as a new challenge, every day as a new discovery—this is the way to live each moment to the fullest.

The American writer and social activist Helen Keller (1880–1968) wrote: "The most important question is not the sort of environment we have, but the kind of thoughts we think every day, the kind of ideals we are following, in a word, the kind of men and women we really are."[8]

Certainly no one is more praiseworthy than the women's division members who uphold the world's supreme philosophy and are dedicating their lives to world peace and the happiness of all humankind.

To my unfailing women's division members, the mothers of kosen-rufu: May you enjoy health, happiness, victory, and glory. And may you create a fresh groundswell of dialogue, an even bigger network of friendships, and a new age of resounding victory for our movement. With all my heart, I salute you!

13 June 2009

(*Kosen-rufu Our Mission,* [New Delhi: Eternal Ganges Press, 2013], vol. 2, 195-201)

Notes:

1. Cf. Adolfo Pérez Esquivel and Daisaku Ikeda, 'Dialogue: Message for the Age of Human Rights—*What Does the Third Millennium Require?* (1),' *The Journal of Oriental Studies,* vol. 17 (October 2007 issue), 30–31.

2.. Cf. Adolfo Pérez Esquivel and Daisaku Ikeda, 'Dialogue: Message for the Age of Human Rights—*What Does the Third Millennium Require?* (2),' *The Journal of Oriental Studies,* vol. 18 (August 2008 issue), 22.

3. Ibid., 23.

4. Ibid.

5. Daisaku Ikeda and Yasushi Inoue, *Letters of Four Seasons,* translated by Richard L. Gage (Tokyo: Kodansha International, 1989), 46.

6. Cf. Margaret Lovell-Smith, *The Woman Question: Writings by the Women who Won the Vote* (Auckland: New Women's Press, 1992), 66.

7. Translated from Japanese. From an article in *Seikyo Shimbun,* 4 April 2009.

8. Helen Keller, *My Religion* (London: Hodder and Stoughton, 1927), 177.

Poems

Waka Poems for the Women's Division

As sunny as a fine May day
The presence of smiling mothers
Will ever tranform
Heaven and earth into a realm of peace and happiness

Like the majestic sun shining from time immemorial
Envelop and warm countless many
With your compassion and love

Mothers of humanity, Do not lament!
Live cheerfully and brightly!
With a lofty philosophy
Life's journey becomes a joy

(*SGI Monthly Newsletter* No. 170, May 1997)

Forever accumulate treasures
in the palace of happiness within your lives,
knowing that the heavenly deities
will protect you as Queens of Kosen-rufu

(*SGI Monthly Newsletter* No. 240, May 2003]

[*Dedicated to my dear, hardworking chapter women's division leaders around the globe whom I hold in the highest esteem, in praise of you valiant efforts to create fresh history in this February Campaign.*]

As mothers
and as partners,
your work selflessly
for the sake of kosen-rufu—
your benefit is everlasting.

As women who champion
the solemn propagation
of the Mystic Law,
you will be staunchly protected
by all Buddhas throughout time and space.

The honour of living a life
of the highest possible value
in this existence
assures the eternal prosperity
of your family and loved ones.

(Value Creation, March 2006, 11)

An ode to mothers,
a paean to mothers,
Everyone should respect and protect
the admirable bodhisattvas
of the women's division.

How noble are our sunny, ever-smiling
women's division members,
who steadfastly cherish
in their hearts
the Buddha's intent and decree.

(Value Creation, March 2007, 30)

The Buddhas and heavenly deities,
will lend their protection
to the noble
mothers of kosen-rufu
as they speak out for justice.

(Value Creation, March 2007, 8)

To the Young Mothers of Kosen-rufu

Young mothers—
how wonderful
and vibrant you are!

Today, again,
you strive with
pure-hearted devotion
to advance kosen-rufu.
How admirable!
How noble!

You pray earnestly
for the health and prosperity
of your families
and the growth and victory
of your children.

You are all
youthful Buddhas
striving wholeheartedly
day after day,

no matter how busy
or how tired you are,
for the happiness of your friends
who are suffering
or in sorrow.

Without a doubt,
you are praised and protected
by the heavenly deities.
This is the law of Buddhism.

With sincerity,
you rush to the aid
of others.
You go out of your way
to find and help
those who are struggling.
And how beautiful is
the heart-to-heart support
and encouragement
you give one another!

What an example
of genuine nobility you are!
In today's hectic world,
how precious is your existence!

The Great Teacher Dengyo,
who transmitted the true spirit

of the Lotus Sutra to Japan,
called those who seek and spread
the Mystic Law
"treasures of the nation."
This distinction
will never change.

The German poet Friedrich von Schiller
said that there can be no higher
and worthier end
than to make people happy.[1]
The efforts of our Soka women
are the most respectworthy
in all the world.

> Wherever you stand up
>   flowers bloom
>   splendidly.

Set forth
into the wide blue sky!
No darkness looms ahead
on your path.

O, young mothers of kosen-rufu!
You are delightful and refreshing,
like a hope-filled spring breeze!
With exuberance and good cheer,
please work together

to further expand
your beautiful network
of friendship.

The French writer
Romain Rolland declared:
"Let us unite
to bring about
a humanistic society
that is more just,
more free, more loving.
Let us struggle
shoulder to shoulder."[2]

A humanistic
gathering of people is needed
to build a humanistic society.
A great alliance
committed to truth and justice
is the unsurpassed way to victory.

My mentor Josei Toda
encouraged young mothers:
"After moving from
the young women's division
into the women's division,
getting married and having children,
you may find yourself swamped
with your new tasks
of homemaking and child rearing.

But to stand up undefeated
and continue growing vigorously
is the mark of genuine faith."
How true this is.

There are people who suffer
over their children,
and some who suffer
over not having children.
Others suffer
over their partner or their family.
And there are many who suffer
over their karma.

"There is no safety
in the threefold world;
it is like a burning house."[3]
It is a harsh reality that
the home,
which should by rights
be a castle of happiness and peace,
is sometimes a burning house
of pain and hardship.
This saha world
is a realm
where such sufferings
must be endured.

But there is no need
for tears of self-pity.

No need to give in
to a self-centred,
pessimistic mind-set.

Ignite the light of courage
in your heart!
Bring the sun of hope
to shine brilliantly within!
Strengthen your inner self!

Nichiren Daishonin declares:
"A hundred years of practice
in the Land of Perfect Bliss
cannot compare to the benefit gained
from one day's practice
in the impure world."[4]
Times of difficulty
enable us to carry out
our Buddhist practice to the full
and accumulate immeasurable benefits.

Not being defeated
is happiness.
Not being defeated
means we are winning.
The Buddhism of the sun
is the driving force
that keeps us going!

In a letter to the lay nun Myoho,
the Daishonin speaks of
"a lantern lighting up a place that has
been dark for a hundred, a thousand,
or ten thousand years."[5]
Indeed, when a woman
who shines like the sun
rises to action,
the dark clouds
hovering over her family
will immediately
disperse and clear.
The light of truth and justice
will glow,
and a garden of good fortune
will unfold.

Nichiren Daishonin
had the deepest trust
in his pure-hearted,
youthful women followers,
whose profound sense of gratitude
towards their mentor
knew no bounds.

In Kamakura,
while the Daishonin
was exiled to Sado,

such harsh persecution
befell his disciples
that 999 out of 1,000
abandoned their faith.[6]
Among them, the elderly Oama,
believed to be the wife
of a large landowner,
showed an utter lack of gratitude
and discarded her faith
at the crucial moment,
despite the immense
support and protection
she had received from the Daishonin.

But though Oama
with her status and authority
made such an about-face,
the faith of her young daughter-in-law,
the virtuous Niiama,
remained unshaken.
Niiama stayed true
even when members of her family
did not.
She followed the path
of a disciple to the end.

The Daishonin praises
the younger woman's faith as
sincere and unwavering.

Young mothers—
you are the central figures
of your families!
You carry the responsibility
of making your home
a magnificent citadel of happiness!
You are a conductor
creating a beautiful melody
of eternal victory!

My wife, too,
devoted herself to activities
as a young mother.
With her children in tow,
she went out regularly
to encourage her friends.

Your appearance
gentle as the moon,
your spirit filled
with the strength
of the Mystic Law.

Mr. Toda
presented this poem to my wife
on his birthday in 1958,[7]
the final year of his life.

During a time
of unrelenting persecution

in the past,
my wife stayed up late
for nights on end,
praying intensely
and honing her insights
into Buddhism
with the resolve that
the time to read the Gosho
was now.

Cold winds and raging blizzards
assailed us day after day.
But together
we continued to advance
with pride and confidence.

I composed this poem for her:

> Husband and wife
>> play the Buddha's melody
>> even in a storm.

The Daishonin
called on his young successors
to dedicate their lives selflessly
to the great vow of kosen-rufu
like "a drop of dew rejoining the ocean".[8]

You,
young mothers,

are creating a peaceful society
for the future.
Burning with hope,
allow your spirits to soar freely.
Open your life
like the vast and boundless sea.

Addressing those in power,
the Dutch thinker Erasmus said that
true leaders are only happy
when they have made their people happy,
and that they will only flourish
when their cities flourish with perpetual peace.[9]
The wise observations
of this great philosopher
have much in common
with the teachings of Buddhism.

What inspired
our friend Betty Williams
to start a grassroots movement
for peace?
It was her outrage
at the brutal violence that had robbed
innocent children of their lives
right before her and her daughter's eyes.

Why did the futurist
Hazel Henderson
become involved

in the environmental movement?
Because she noticed
how heavily polluted the air was
upon discovering soot
on her daughter's skin
whenever she came home from school.

It is the call for justice
of young mothers,
their actions fueled
by righteous anger,
that sets in motion
such significant movements—
these networks of mothers
working together
with a wish for
the welfare and happiness
of future generations.

Arrogant people
may sneer.
But their words are nothing
but meaningless taunts.

Fear nothing!
Never forget that
fearlessness
is a sign

of being an expert
in the art of happiness.

Fear nothing!
To fear nothing
is the first step to
attaining genuine happiness.
It is the manifestation
of firm conviction
gained through Buddhist practice.

Society
is concerned with reputation.
Government
is concerned with reward and punishment.
Buddhism
is concerned with winning.
Indeed,
life is a struggle
that we must win.

It is foolish
to be overly concerned
with the judgments of others.
All that matters
is that you yourself
continue to triumph joyously.

Young mothers—
you are the front runners

in our effort to bring about
a century of respect
for the sanctity of life.

In our dialogue,
the African environmentalist
Dr. Wangari Maathai
asserted with a smile:
"If you want change,
you must first change yourself.
I believe that life
is a wonderful experience
that we should enjoy."

Gazing up at the rainbow-filled
sky of the future,
patiently continue
making golden efforts!
The flowers of happiness
of mothers and children
bloom fragrantly
in the earth of perseverance.

Never isolate yourself from others.
You have friends
from time immemorial.
You have a mission
from the eternal past.

My wife and I
are always
earnestly praying and
sending daimoku for
your safety and security,
your good health and long life,
your happiness and victory.

The inspiring Helen Keller
offered this noble creed:
"I believe
we should act
so that we may draw nearer
and more near
the age when no man
shall live at his ease
while another suffers."[10]

She also said:
"And there
is yet another
on which all depends—
to bear this faith
above every tempest which overfloods it,
and to make it a principle in disaster
and through affliction."[11]

The cause of good advances
when you take a courageous step forward.

Future victory lies
in your tireless efforts.

The Daishonin declares:
"There is no true happiness for human beings
other than chanting Nam-myoho-renge-kyo."[12]
And:
"Suffer what there is to suffer,
Enjoy what there is to enjoy.
Regard both suffering and joy as facts of life,
and continue chanting Nam-myoho-renge-kyo,
no matter what happens."[13]

Those who strive in faith
and fight on to the very end
savor genuine happiness.

"The greater the hardships
befalling [the votary of the Lotus Sutra],
the greater the delight he feels,
because of his strong faith,"[14]
states the Daishonin.

Those who persevere in faith
through all manner of
difficulties and challenges
are certain to attain Buddhahood.

Such people will become
invincible monarchs of happiness.
This is a law of life
and the teaching
of Buddhism.

Fine sentiments may be uttered
by celebrities,
but that is all they are.
They hold no candle
to the messages of the eternal leaders
Shakyamuni and Nichiren Daishonin.

Words
are the lifeblood of Buddhism.
Truly,
"the voice does the Buddha's work."[15]

Words brimming with compassion,
words refuting error,
words engaging others
in pleasant conversation,
and words defeating
devilish functions—
the words of the Buddha
are the words of the universe.
They embody the law of life
and the simultaneity
of cause and effect.
They are eternal and unchanging

words of philosophy
expressing the fundamental Law
of the universe,
just as it is.

Young mothers
who possess a noble mission!
Exert yourselves joyfully again today
in your efforts to speak with others
about the great teaching of Buddhism!

For the sake of your own life!
For the sake of your family!
And for the sake of a triumphant life
lived without regret!

From you,
from your communities,
a new age will emerge
in which the bright, unadorned voices
and smiling faces of mothers and children
will be found in every corner of the world!

Your efforts will establish
happiness and truth for all!
They will realise
a humanistic world without war!
They will achieve
lasting peace!
And they will bring

the dignity of each precious life
to shine with unsurpassed brilliance!

11 February 2007
Commemorating the birthday
of my mentor Josei Toda.

Mentor-Disciple Hall
Soka Gakkai Headquarters
Daisaku Ikeda

(*Value Creation,* April 2007, 11-29)

Notes:

1. Friedrich von Schiller, 'On the Use of the Chorus in Tragedy,' in *Schiller's Complete Works*, translated by Charles J. Hempel (Philadelphia: I. Kohler, 1861), vol. 1, 452.

2. Translated from French. Edmond Privat and Romain Rolland, *Bon Voisinage* (Good Neighborliness) (Switzerland: Editions de la Baconnière, 1977), 186.

3. LSOC3, 69.

4. 'On Repaying Debts of Gratitude', WND-1, 736.

5. 'The One Essential Phrase', WND-1, 923.

6. Cf. 'Reply to Niiama', WND-1, 469.

7. February 11.

8. 'The Dragon Gate', WND-1, 1003.

9. Cf. Erasmus, *The Complaint of Peace* (New York: Scholars' Facsimiles and Reprints, 1946), 40.

10. Helen Keller, *Optimism: An Essay* (New York: T.Y. Crowell and Company, 1903), 75.

11. Ibid., 75–76.

12. 'Happiness in This World', WND-1, 681.

13. Ibid.

14. 'A Ship to Cross the Sea of Suffering', WND-1, 33.

15. Cf. OTT, 4.

A Symphony of Great and Noble Mothers

—Dedicated to the Gentle, Wise, and Courageous
Mothers of Kosen-rufu

Mothers
have
beautiful
resolute hearts.
The nobility of mothers
lies not in their appearance or clothing,
nor in their social status or possessions,
nor in the size of their home,
nor in the spaciousness of their garden.

Mothers are the sun,
brightest of all.
Mothers are the earth,
infinitely bountiful.
Mothers are the symbols of happiness,
ever optimistic,
walking tall with their heads held high.

Mothers dedicated to truth and justice
are never intimidated
by jealous
or malicious attacks
aimed at them.

Even if they do not have
a prestigious educational background,
even if they are treated badly
or spoken ill of,
even if no one lavishes attention on them
like celebrities,
wise mothers
remain unaffected.

No matter
how illustrious
or famous
a person's ancestors or relatives may be,
they cannot compete
with the gentle hearts of mothers.
Buddhism teaches:
"It is the heart that is important",[1] and
"Fortune comes from one's heart
and makes one worthy of respect."[2]
The heart
is the foundation for happiness.

Caring nothing
for social status or wealth,
today again,
true to their beliefs,
mothers steadfastly
pray for others;
today again,
they give their all
to support and help others.

The American poet of the people
Walt Whitman,
whom I have loved from my youth,
praised mothers:
"Some of the old women, the mothers:
no one ever hears of them!

But they are the salt of the earth:
noble, courageous, disinterested —
not to be forgotten in any count
of the great national, great world, forces."[3]
How true this is!

Even when bitter days
follow one after another,
days when their sincere efforts
are scorned by others,
mothers
press onward
undaunted

on the path of truth and justice,
the path of happiness,
the path of peace.

Mothers!
When I see the word
"mother",
emotion overcomes me;
when I hear the word
"mother",
my heart aches,
yet it also soars!
So exclaimed a philosopher.

That same one said:
"If people the world over,
without exception,
treasured mothers,
peace would be realised
as a matter of course,
a path to happiness would be paved,
a joyous procession would ensue."

Yes!
Cherishing mothers —
that is
the surest course,
shining with sun-like brilliance,
for achieving peace and happiness,
progress and development.

Nichiren Daishonin
solemnly declares:
"Hell
is in the heart of a person
who . . . disregards his mother."[4]

The hearts of those
who disparage mothers,
who disregard them,
and cause them suffering,
are already blanketed
in the darkness of hell.

People of deplorable arrogance
who insult mothers!
Domineering authorities
who persecute mothers!
None are
more spiritually bereft,
more base-hearted,
or do more to destroy others' happiness.

Cruel, callous individuals
who threaten mothers,
who upset mothers,
who debase mothers,
who harm mothers!
None in the world
are more reprehensible,
for they destroy

peaceful and happy societies.
So declared
a renowned educator.

Don't make mothers suffer!
Protect mothers!
Praise mothers!
Don't belittle mothers!
Give mothers
all your support and love.
That is the way of humanity.
Poets,
scientists,
and authors
have all asserted this.
I agree.
One day,
a disciple of the Buddha
spoke of how ignorant his mother was.
His teacher Shakyamuni
sternly rebuked him:
"Who gave birth
to this body of yours?
It was your mother who did so."[5]

All people
are born from mothers.
Mothers
risk their lives
giving birth to us.

The *Orally Transmitted Teachings* states:
"The Treasure Purity World
[the earth from which the Treasure Tower emerges[6]]
is the womb of our mothers."[7]
No entities
are more precious than
    mothers
who lovingly nurture life.

Mother, beloved mother!
Even now,
when I think of my mother,
a powerful emotion fills my heart.
I wanted
to do more for her.
I wanted
to take better care of her.

Oh admirable mothers!
Mothers who,
in spite of poverty,
survived,
endured,
and lived out their lives
with grace and strength,
leaving this world
with a feeling of deep satisfacti‹
Let our tears
express our gratitude
and praise for them,

and let us reflect
upon our attitudes towards them.

My mother's name
was Ichi —
meaning "one", "best" or "greatest".
Her parents named her that
with the wish that she would find
the greatest happiness.
They also hoped
that her own children
would be the best
in their chosen field
and contribute to society.

World War II
dragged her four oldest sons,
the mainstays of the family,
to the battlefield.
My mother,
together with my father,
pleaded:
"Isn't it enough
to take one son from a family
and send him off to war?
In some families
no one is taken.
We sent four sons
off to fight."

Her eldest son
died in the conflict
in Burma
at the young age of.[29]

During the war,
women were praised
as "war mothers",
but
in the dark days of defeat,
in a complete about-face,
they were insulted
as parents of idiot soldiers
who had brought the nation to ruin.

War cruelly
made mothers
weep in despair.

But
my elderly mother
of humble means
always
wore a smile.

Watching me, her son,
fighting for peace and justice,
her smile stayed with her
to the very end,

knowing that she had triumphed.
What happens along the way is not important.
What matters is how magnificently
we can adorn the final season of our life.

Based on the law of life
pervading the cycle of
birth, ageing, sickness, and death,
and caressed by the breezes of
eternity, happiness, true self, and purity,
mothers
are great victors
and masters in the art of living.

Offering our deepest respect to mothers
and repaying
our enormous debt of gratitude to them
should be the foundation of education
and the essence of government.
Indeed, this spirit
is the joyous light
of world peace.

None are more base and foolish
than those who treat their parents badly.
They may appear splendid,
but their hearts are ruled by the world of Animality.
None have achieved true greatness
without valuing their parents.

Many are those who have gone on to greatness,
after making amends to their parents
for previous neglect.

Looking down on one's parents
is spiritual defeat!
Treasuring one's parents
is a victory of the heart!

No matter how challenging
their lives may appear,
those who cherish their mothers
can advance
with pride and dignity,
forever with their mothers
on the golden path of happiness.

When my mentor Josei Toda was 19 years old,
he encountered his mentor Tsunesaburo Makiguchi.
As he prepared to leave his hometown
in Hokkaido
for Tokyo,
his mother presented him
with a quilted padded jacket
she had lovingly made him,
saying:
"If you wear this as you work,
no matter how difficult things may be,
you can accomplish anything."

After his release
from two years of imprisonment
for his beliefs,
Mr Toda donned that jacket again.
An indomitable spirit burned within him,
knowing that as long as he had this jacket,
everything would be all right.

Nothing is stronger
than the armour of a mother's love.
We develop and grow in strength
by responding to
our mother's hopes for us.
No matter how difficult life may be,
to think of our mother
and do our very best
is to repay our gratitude to her.

A mother of kosen-rufu is a mother,
even if she has no children of her own.
She is a mother,
even if she has no partner.

Dr. Sarah Wider,
former president of
the Ralph Waldo Emerson Society,
remarked that
we are living in a society
that has all but forgotten motherhood.

We need to
once again
foster a profound spirit
of genuine respect for mothers.

No matter
how convenient
or comfortable our lives become,
or how advanced our society grows,
if we forget the importance
of all that motherhood stands for,
we will be nothing but ungrateful barbarians
trampling on the earth that gives birth to life.

Nichiren Daishonin
declared unequivocally:
"Since I have realised
that only the Lotus Sutra teaches
the attainment of Buddhahood by women,
and that only the Lotus
is the sutra of true requital
for repaying the kindness of our mother,
in order to repay my debt
to my mother,
I have vowed to enable all women
to chant the daimoku of this sutra."[8]

Dedicating ourselves
to the noble mission of kosen-rufu
is the supreme way to repay our gratitude

to our own beloved mothers
as well as
all the noble mothers of the world,
following the example of the Daishonin.
Here we find the revitalising light
of joy and vigour
that allows us to live with
utmost humanity and dignity.

February marks the birthdays
of the Daishonin
and my mentor Mr Toda.
It is also a month
for remembering
the great mothers
who raised these towering individuals.

During the February Campaign,[9]
when I stood up resolutely
to respond to my mentor's aspirations
at the age of 24,
I pledged together with
the hardworking mothers of Kamata:

First,
we will begin with prayer.
Second,
we will treasure
our community and society.
Third,

we will enthusiastically
share our experiences in faith with our friends.

Following this formula,
we chanted earnestly;
we tirelessly engaged in dialogue;
and we acted with great sincerity and commitment.

The February Campaign,
which opened the way
for the present tremendous development
of worldwide kosen-rufu,
was a drama
of the victory of utterly dedicated mothers.

"There is no such thing as retreat
for a [person] of prayer."[10]
These are the words
of Mahatma Gandhi.

Nothing is stronger
than mothers' prayers.
Nothing can beat
the actions of mothers
who chant to the Gohonzon
and are giving their all.

No matter how
the three powerful enemies

or three obstacles and four devils assailed us,
the mothers of Soka
always remained optimistic,
deeply prepared for any circumstance:
"It is all just as written in the Gosho.
We will not be defeated!"

Chanting wholeheartedly,
chanting till victory was theirs,
and always smiling brightly,
they brimmed with good cheer
and positive energy
as they declared:
"We have won!"
"How wonderful!"

Their awe-inspiring smiles,
their vibrant voices
fill me only with the deepest
respect and veneration.
How intensely
they chanted for our success!
How tenaciously
they continued chanting to the end!

The 80 years of the Soka Gakkai
have been victorious because of mothers' prayers!
The 50 years of fierce struggle of the third president
has been triumphant because of mothers' prayers!

"Mother"
means someone who is never defeated;
it is another word for a person
who is guaranteed to win in the end.

Louisa May Alcott,
author of *Little Women*, wrote:
"Giving joy and peace to others
brings it fourfold to us,
bearing a double happiness
in the blessings
to those we help."[11]

What kind of woman
is genuinely noble?
A woman
who can speak the truth
boldly and fearlessly
to the most arrogant
and self-important people,
a woman who
reaches out equally
to all who are suffering
and gives hope and inspiration.

The world
is now praising
the mothers of Soka,
comparing them to orchids.

Since ancient times,
the orchid has been considered
to be among the most lofty
and beautiful
of all blossoms.

Fragrant,
fresh,
lovely,
refined and elegant,
sublime and pure —
it is the queen
of flowers.

Widely admired
like the orchid,
the network for peace
of the mothers of Soka
is actively promoting
friendship and dialogue,
with each member epitomising
what the Daishonin calls
"a friend in the orchid room,"[12]
positively influencing others
with their lofty virtue.

The Daishonin declares:
"One added to one
becomes two,

two becomes three,
and so on to make ten, a hundred,
a thousand, ten thousand,
a hundred thousand, or an asamkhya.[13]
Yet 'one'
is the mother of all."[14]

Everything
starts from one person.
It starts from a mother's spirit
of caring for a single individual.

Mothers!
Great and noble
mothers of Soka!
May you
who are gentle and wise,
strong and true, like Buddhas,
courageously and masterfully
conduct a grand symphony
of triumphant happiness
resounding high into the heavens!

To the members of the women's division
who are working so hard for kosen-rufu:
Take care of your health!
Live long!
Have happy family lives!
Be energetic!

I pray that, as experts in the art of happiness
and genuine winners,
you will lead lives of fulfilment
adorned with wonderful blessings.
Three cheers for the mothers of kosen-rufu!
Three cheers for the mothers of Soka!
Three cheers for the mothers of peace!
Three cheers for the mothers of victory!

9 February 2009
Daisaku Ikeda
At the Mentor-Disciple Hall, Soka Gakkai
Headquarters

(*Value Creation,* April 2009, 17-34)

Notes:

1. 'The Strategy of the Lotus Sutra', WND-1, 1000.

2. 'New Year's Gosho', WND-1, 1137.

3. Horace Traubel, *With Walt Whitman in Camden*, edited by Jeanne Chapman and Robert MacIsaac (Carbondale, Illinois: Southern Illinois University Press, 1992), vol. 7, 304.

4. 'New Year's Gosho', WND-1, 1137.

5. 'A Mother's Gift of a Robe', WND-2, 532.

6. Cf. OTT, 228-29.

7. OTT, 91.

8. 'The Sutra of True Requital', WND-1, 931.

9. February Campaign: In February 1952, President Ikeda, then an advisor to Tokyo's Kamata Chapter, initiated a dynamic propagation campaign. Together with the Kamata members, he broke through the previous monthly record of some 100 new member households by introducing the Daishonin's Buddhism to 201 new member households.

10. Mahatma Gandhi, *The Collected Works of Mahatma Gandhi* (New Delhi: Publications Division, Ministry of Information and Broadcasting, Government of India, 1970), vol. 38 (November 1928–February 1929), 248.

11. Louisa May Alcott, *Flower Fables* (Great Neck, New York: Core Collection Books, Inc., 1977), 146.

12. 'On Establishing the Correct Teaching for the Peace of the Land', WND-1, 23.

13. Asamkhya: A numerical unit of ancient India used to indicate an exceedingly large number.

14. 'The Blessings of the Lotus Sutra', WND-1, 667.

The 21st Century is the Century of Women

The 21st Century is the Century of Women—
With Deep Appreciation for All the Noble
Mothers of the World

—Praying for the Happiness of all Women

I know
And you know
The secret
To why we were born with a shared destiny
As human beings
And became friends of profound connection
And comrades in faith.

In our own unique way,
You and I
Strive to fulfill
The wondrous dream

And the wondrous mission
That pervade our lives
Across eternity.

We decisively embrace hope,
We feel no anxiety,
Toiling with every ounce of our beings,
Our hearts sing,
We who have stood up
For world peace
For a philosophy of happiness
Based on the eternity of life.

Though nameless ordinary people,
We will be remembered in history
Under the noble name,
Victory.

My home
ls humble, but
lt is one of true humanity.
Filled with many resolute dreams.
This is
My greatest source of pride.

I have no need
To look in a clouded mirror
With the power to change my karma,
A bright future awaits me;

Once coloured by a bleak outlook on life
The past and all its attendant sufferings
Have now vanished.

l am living my life.
I am free of anguished dreams.
With high spirits,
I live in and gaze upon
A beautiful earthly kingdom.

l have many
Wonderful friends,
l have many
Wonderful books

My life is removed
From the pitiful self-conceited
Not for me
A life of vanity
That brings only darkness.
I will not fall into those insidious
Hidden traps.

We who gravitate toward happiness and good
Are greeted by friends who sympathise with our ideals,
Always respecting the beauty within us,
And by a paradise tremulous with hope.

Our doubt and anxiety
Toward a society rife with contradictions

Have been replaced by an unshakeable faith
That we have always longed for.
We have won!

Our unimaginably painful struggles
Have also given way
To a state of life
In which we gaze upon all from a lofty height.

Nichiren Daishonin writes:
"A woman who embraces
The lion king of the Lotus Sutra
Never fears any of the beasts of hell
Or of the realms of hungry spirits and animals."[1]

We are saddened
That many people
Lead miserable existences,
Allowing themselves
To be dragged about
In the pitch-black darkness of delusion,
Slavishly following force of habit.

Our lives
Are always a vibrant dawn.
They are a realm
Of mothers' youthful affection.
Forever hearkening to morning's song
Drenched in golden sunlight
And golden rain.

The eternal and unique power of mothers.
Their great presence
Is more powerfully attractive
Than any adventurer.
Women are truth incarnate
Mothers are victory personified.

No matter how they may be deceived
Or attacked by devilish forces,
They command the power to,
In the end, adamantly indict the offender,
With mental wheels of wisdom ever spinning,
They possess the courage to see through deception
This awe-inspiring beauty
Is the strength of mothers, of women,
That fills their lives with happiness.

Come!
The century of women
Has dawned,
The sun rises on the horizon.
Instead of the pallid,
Dim light of old,
Now the fiercely burning sun
Has begun to light the way ahead
For these extraordinary mothers.

These praiseworthy mothers
Must never be imprisoned
By the iron bars of misery.

Let us all live noble lives,
Brimming with golden affection,
Comforting these mothers in their loneliness
And strongly supporting and protecting each other!
Let us make mothers the queens
Of this empire of supreme happiness

And
With a stylus,
Let us inscribe an epitaph
In tribute to these mothers
As great immortal nameless actors.

O the century of women!
Now we close the curtain
On a long history of misfortune,
Letting it sink
Beneath the tides of time,
And allowing a drama
Of genuine human happiness
To unfold without end.

Repeatedly
Throughout past ages,
An unjustifiable history
Of sadness
Has flowed continuously,
Like so much flotsam,
In the beautiful hearts of mothers.

No matter what insult
We suffer in society,
Our vision is
To vanquish without fail
The shadowy knaves of hell
And create everywhere
A world abloom with the flowers
Of love and laughter
Of mothers, those heavenly beings.

There are people who grow jealous
At the sight of others' wealth.
Jealousy has the power
Of a devil's sword
To make people unhappy,

There are those who grow jealous
At the sight of mothers enjoying success,
And who resort to spreading false rumours,
Inflicting pain and anguish
On these golden-hearted ones,

But
Mothers are made of greater substance,
They possess a profound, abiding strength
That is why
They pay no heed
To petty rumours or malicious gossip.

We must change this base, arrogant,
Almost insane society in which we live,
And
With a new spirit,
With a new philosophy,
Create an age
Which eternally honours mothers,
This
Is the century of women,
A wise person said.

Even if they are poor,
Even if they are sick,
Even if they have lost their partners,
In the dauntless hearts of mothers,
Citadels of happiness and victory
Are forged.

Nichiren Daishonin said:
"The woman who upholds the Lotus Sutra
Is like clear water,
In which the moon of Shakyamuni Buddha
Is reflected"[2]

Mothers!
Clever mothers,
Mothers!
Gentle mothers.
Mothers!

Unlearned mothers.
Mothers!
Nagging mothers,
Mothers!
Wise mothers,
Mothers!
Mothers of strong faith,
Mothers!
Unaffected and talkative mothers.

But
In the hearts of mothers
Who have been buffeted by storms,
There is always
Fresh and passionate
Determination and love
Born of profound life experience.

Mothers unadorned
By expensive jewels-
Who instead wear only
A simple brooch,
Far from regal,
Yet rich in sentimental value.

Even so,
Stroking
Their children's heads,
They possess the beauty of triumph,

Ever shining,
Far surpassing a life of misery,
And even more a life of folly.

Mothers!
You are great uncrowned queens of
Living with a firm purpose
That nothing can destroy—
A life which shines
With awesome beauty.

The youthfulness ofa mother
Who turns up at a meeting
In a hastily borrowed blouse
Of her daughters

The endearing mother who,
After borrowing her daughter's high heels
With a quick "I'm sorry",
Rushes to a meeting,
Only to complain for a week after
About how much her feet hurt!
Yet she doesn't make a single complaint
About not being able to afford
A new pair of shoes for herself,
She lives so frugally
That it is touching.

Late returning from a meeting,
She is scolded unreasonably by her partner,
But she retains her dignity
And defends herself ably, saying:
"It's for the sake of justice and our good fortune"—
With a skill outrivalling
Any politician on the House floor.

The confident spirit of a mother,
Who is the embodiment of love itself.
Like the Count of Monte Cristo,
She finally draws an admission from her partner.
"All right, all right, I was wrong."
A mother whom all praise
As being more eloquent
Than any prime minister.

Though her partner the scholar,
Her son the student,
And her daughter the genius,
Start out thinking they can beat
Her in an argument,
In the end

They are no match
For her intelligence and wisdom.

The proud mother retorts:
"That is an argument
You've learned somewhere,

But it is not real life.
It has no flesh or blood.
Words you've read are just pouring
From your heads,
I am waging a real-life struggle
For survival
In daily life,
In actual society.
That's why l am strong."

As Goethe said:
"Trust in life!
It teaches us more
Than any orator or book can?"[3]
How true!

Mothers
Are fearless.
They are invincible victors
Who have won the quintessential triumph
Of the human spirit.
A famous poet asserted
That this formula—
In every time and place—
ls the hidden essence of
Human history.

Though a mother may
Be bedridden, exhausted and feverish,

She says to others,
"Please take care."
Though no one pampers her,
She encourages
Her partner and children, and her friends.
How noble these actions of the Bodhisattva!

The infinite strength of mothers who,
Even if they have lost their partners,
Live courageously,
Like the immortal phoenix,
Working actively
Amid the harsh realities of society.
Children grow up
Looking at the example of their mothers:
That is without a doubt
An eternal truth.

The century of women
Is truly a period
Of the ripening of democracy.
Elections are the first step
To the sovereignty of the people.
Elections are the right of all citizens
And their duty.

For the sake of kosen-rufu as well,
For the unbounded expansion
Of those who share our ideals,

Let us carry out a cheerful struggle
To redraw the face
Of Japan.

Mothers, living in the real world,
Work tirelessly to advocate our cause,
Talking cheerfully about many issues.
A learned scholar has praised their efforts
As a movement to realise
True sovereignty of the people.

Seemingly foolish yet wise mothers.
Seemingly cranky yet pure-hearted mothers,
Mothers who, though on occasion
Incur people's dislike,
Can be counted on in a crisis.
Mothers who put on airs
But privately reflect on their own folly.

Mothers whose lives are modest
But whose hearts
Are as rich as billionaires
Mothers who are like queens.
Mothers who, deceived by seemingly valid arguments
Despite glaring contradictions,
Stubbornly set about proving
The righteousness of their position,

And mothers without children,
They too are not lonely in the least, exclaiming:

"1 have so many friends;
There are so many young people in my life
Who will carry on in the future."

And, with cheerful laughter,
They say serenely:
"There are too many people in Japan,
Too many people on our planet.
We don`t need so many people!"

When mother is in a good mood,
Everyone is bright and happy,
Like the sun.
When mother is irritated,
It is like a sad and lonely night
Lashed by cold winds and heavy rain,

Glad when her children`s grades go up,
Sad when her children`s grades go down
But in the end, she gives up and,
Turning the report card upside down,
Smiles and says with humor,
"Now *these* are good grades!"

Mothers who know
The rules for living
Honest and decent lives
With a spirit of generosity, enthusiasm
And diligence.

Mothers who treasure
Boys and girls who have no hope or love
As if they were her own.
And life's quintessential mothers,
Always strict yet compassionate,
Who, when children are suffering
Through disaster or disease,
Search for the cause
And fight against inhumanity

The compassion of mothers
Who can love
Children who have lost hope
And been abandoned by society
As if they were their own,

Idealistic mothers
Filled with courage
Who, like great liberators,
Extend staunch protection to children
Who have fallen into cruel, human hells.

These uncrowned mothers
Are far, far greater
Than those who stand
In the vanguard of the revolutions
Of the world's renowned thinkers,
They are greater
Than any eminent political leader,

Yet nations do not bestow
Upon these mothers
Even a single medal

O the courage of mothers
Who carry out orderly humanitarian efforts
In the cause of justice,
Naturally and without pretension,
On the world stage.

A certain distinguished educator noted
That even the president of a country
Has the highest respect for mothers.
l agree.
This is life.
This is humanity.
Those whose hearts
Are ruled by Animality
Are pitiful wretches
Who have strayed
From the path of humanity.

Mothers who are natural pacifists,
Opposed to war.
Mothers who hate cruel deception.
O the inner flame of love
With which mothers make their way
Through life's sorrows and disappointments,
Hurt by their partners,
Or weeping over the delinquency of their children!

The vast, expansive realm
Of Buddhahood,
That enables all mothers
To lead truly happy lives
Is a global, borderless nation
Of genuine happiness.

There can be no discrimination
Among mothers.
Just because one lives in a luxurious house,
Or has money,
Or social status,
Or one's children are smart,
Or one's partner has a prestigious job,
Or one has a noble lineage—
All such things
Are completely irrelevant,

Being alive
Is itself
The greatest joy.
This is true happiness.
This is a mother's wish.

Not wealth.
Not honours.
Not vanity.
Not fame.
Not social status.

A true mother—
No matter how humble her existence,
Her love as a mother
Shines.
This is an eternal
And indestructible treasure.

There are occasionally
Mothers
Who commit terrible acts,
But this springs from immaturity;
It is not the true reality of motherhood.

Children
Respect their mothers
When they see
The beautiful way they exert themselves
On behalf of others in society,

Mothers
Are the primeval sun,
And
Our deceased mothers
Are always alive in our hearts.
We converse with them
Throughout our lives.

Mothers desire
A world of eternal harmony and peace.
In Buddhism,

This is called kosen-rufu,
To achieve this
The Soka Gakkai women's division members
Have launched a momentous struggle.

The history
Of this strong and beautiful alliance
Now marks its glorious 50th year,
Now marks its proud 50th anniversary.

At times scolded by their seniors,
At times teased by their juniors,
At times criticised by people in their community,
At times abused by their next-door neighbours,
At times ridiculed by their old school friends
As "religious fanatics"—
Amidst all this,
They have worked tirelessly
To realise world peace,
The dream of all humanity.
This is the reality
Of our noble and lofty women's division members

If the Buddha's teachings are true,
How highly these hardworking women
Must be praised
By all Buddhas and bodhisattvas
Throughout the three existences
And ten directions.
The citadel of life that brings

Eternal prosperity, glory and victory
To their families and relatives
Is without a doubt
Everlasting and indestructible.

I have won
You have won.
We have definitely won!
That is the declaration
Of Nichiren Daishonin and Shakyamuni Buddha.

We do not need
The praise of fools.
We do not need
The praise of the envious.
The wonderful praise
Of the Buddhas and heavenly deities
Is shining brightly,
Enfolding our mothers' lives
In its brilliant illumination.

Our mothers are strong,
Our mothers are wise,
Our mothers have won!

8 May, 2001
In commemoration of Mother 's Day
And the 50th anniversary of the women's division

Poet Laureate

(Translated from the 10 May, 2001 issue of *Seikyo Shimbun*,
the Soka Gakkai daily newspaper)

Notes:

1.   'The Drum at the gate of Thunder', WND-1, 949.

2.   GZ, 1395.

3.   Translated from German. Wolfgang von Goethe, *Goethe Gedichte* (Goethe Poems) ed
     Heinz Nicolai (Frankfurt am Main: Insel Verlag, 1982, 417).

Words to Live By

[M]OST PEOPLE FEEL that as long as a woman gets married and her husband makes his mark in the world then she is complete, or that it doesn't make any difference what happens to her as long as her children grow up and "make it" in society.

This is supposedly the attitude of the virtuous mother and wife. Such a woman abandons efforts to grow as a human being and loses respect for herself and for her personality. The woman who has lost the awareness of herself as an individual and the desire to grow may be thanked for all that she has done but her ability to inspire respect from her children for her once attractive personality vastly diminishes. . . . What I want for all women, particularly young women starting out in life, is for them never to lose their identity. Very soon after a woman is married she tends to lose that vitality, that liveliness with which she once made all around her happy. . . .

In order to maintain life as an individual with a clear-cut identity requires an unusual degree of struggle and concentrated effort. Devotion to purpose is what brings out in the individual the captivating charm of a human being. . . . The wife, principal actor in the home, must always maintain pride in herself as well as love for her family. As a happy by-product, the husband will feel a limitless fascination, finding a wealth of personality in that woman who is his wife.

NICHIREN DAISHONIN SAYS: "It is the power of the bow that determines the flight of the arrow, the might of the dragon that controls the movement of the clouds and the strength of the wife that guides the actions of her husband" ('The Bow and Arrow', WND-1, 656). These words emphasise just how important women are in their families and their communities.

I would like you to always be the shining sun of your family. No matter what storms of adversity you may encounter, please chant daimoku resolutely to overcome them all. And please be women of great wisdom who help their husbands apply themselves fully to their work and also to their Gakkai activities. At the same time, I hope you will be good mothers and friends to your children, aware of your responsibility to raise them with love and understanding to become capable leaders of the future.

WOMEN BRIGHTEN THE home. A woman just has to decide, "As long as I'm around, any situation will be a bright one." If we ourselves become a "sun", there will be no darkness in the world. If there is one person in the home who is like a sun, the entire family will be illuminated. All we need to do is become a person overflowing with good fortune who shares his or her boundless fortune with the family.

I FIND a woman's face weathered from numerous storms in life to be beautiful. No matter what her age, just like the beauty of grains on wood that deepens with passage of time, beauty that has endured hardships shines with a distinctive splendour. . . .A woman who can praise, appreciate and wholeheartedly respect those around her is more beautiful than another who is constantly criticising others. In the same way, someone who can find joy and excitement of her own in her daily life, or even in nature and the changes of the seasons, has the warmth and brightness that can give a sense of peace and comfort to others. Being an expert in discovering beauty makes one beautiful.

THIS BUDDHISM HAS the power to transform your suffering into happiness, to change the tears you have shed into glittering jewels of good fortune. Those who have wept the most bitterly have the right to become the happiest people of all. . . .I'm sure you're all wondering whether you can really become happy through this practice. . . .There's absolutely nothing to worry about. So long as you persevere in your practice, each of you, without exception, can become happy.

NICHIREN DAISHONIN SAID:
"A woman who upholds the Lotus Sutra
Is like pure water;
The moon of Shakyamuni Buddha will reside there."
('The Buddha Resides in a Pure Heart', WND-2, 885)

IT MAY BE lonely being the only person practising in your family, but if you exert yourself diligently, your benefit and good fortune will extend to and be shared by your entire family. Your presence will be just like a huge umbrella sheltering them from the rain. . . .

The most fundamental thing is for each of you to demonstrate the greatness of faith with your own life. . . . Continue to strive in faith as wives and mothers, growing as human beings and becoming sunny presences overflowing with good cheer, wisdom, warmth and consideration.

IT IS TRUE Buddhism teaches that one who commits evil deeds against others will receive the negative effects of those actions and live an unhappy life. ... [But] the Buddhism of Nichiren Daishonin goes far beyond the framework of superficial causality. It elucidates the most fundamental cause and shows us the means for returning to the pure life within that has existed since time without beginning. This fundamental cause is to awaken to our mission as Bodhisattvas of the Earth and dedicate our lives to the widespread propagation of the Law.

Buddhism teaches that its practitioners "voluntarily choose to be born in evil circumstances so they may help others". This means that although we have accumulated the benefit, through our Buddhist practise, to be born in favourable circumstances, we have purposely chosen to be born in the midst of suffering people and there propagate the Mystic Law. For example, if someone who had always lived like a queen and enjoyed every luxury were to say "I became happy as a result of taking faith," no one would bat an eye. But if a person who is sick, whose family is poor, and who is shunned by people because of these things becomes happy through practising faith and goes on to become a leader in society, this will be splendid proof of the greatness of Buddhism.

By triumphing over great poverty, a person who has been poor can give hope to others who are struggling with financial hardship. By regaining vitality and good health, someone who has been battling illness can light a flame of courage in the hearts of those in similar straits. By creating a happy and harmonious family, a person who has suffered great anguish over discord in the home can become a model for others plagued by family problems.

THE TIMES ARE changing. Countries and organisations that recognise and value women and their contributions will flourish.

THE CONVERSATION OF women of keen perception who are sensitive to the feelings of others has the power to open even the most heavily barricaded heart. It is invariably women's cries for justice that move people to action and change the times.

WHEN WE TAKE a long-range view, over a period of 20 or 30 years, those families where the wife's faith is weak are somehow unable to build a solid foundation of security and happiness. In contrast, when a wife has received training in faith, and her practice is solid, her entire family will accumulate fortune as time goes on and her husband's faith will also be stable.

MY MOTHER WAS an ordinary Japanese woman like many other women born in the late 19th century. She devoted herself to her rather difficult husband and raised eight children, seven boys and one girl. I was the fifth son. There were also two adopted children, a total of 10. Her life was by no means an easy one. . . .She drew on her inner strength and endlessly gave for the sake of her family in an extremely tough environment. She used to call us the "champions of poverty", and she always stayed cheerful, never complaining. Whatever I was going through, her presence gave me great hope and courage.

My mother's words are permanently engraved on my heart. . . . The words that I remember most are not extraordinary: "Don't do anything that causes others trouble" and "Don't tell lies." When we began school she added: "Once you decide to do something, take responsibility for it and carry it out yourself."

I also learned from her actions. In spite of the large number of children she had to cope with, in everything, from dividing the food to the settling of quarrels, she showed fairness and impartiality. She was in fact a highly skilled judge and arbitrator.

THOUGH COSMETICS CAN be applied to the face, one cannot gloss over the face of the soul. The law of cause and effect functioning in the depths of life is strict and impartial. . . .In the world of Buddhism, one never fails to receive an effect for one's actions—whether for good or bad; therefore, it is meaningless to be two-faced or to try to put on airs. The "face of the soul" that is carved out by the good and evil causes one makes is to an extent reflected in one's appearance. . . .Just as you look into a mirror when you make up your face, to beautify "the face of the soul" you need a mirror that reflects the depths of your life. This mirror is none other than the Gohonzon of "observing one's mind", or more precisely, observing one's life.

I [WANT] MEMBERS of the women's division to become experts in happiness and daily life. Steering your families on a course towards happiness like so many accomplished pilots, please become the radiant "flowers" and "suns" of the SGI.

(*Value Creation*, August 2007, 172-77)